Prediabetes Weight Loss Solution

PREDIABETES WEIGHT LOSS SOLUTION

Reverse Your Diagnosis and Reclaim Your Health

Manuel Villacorta, RD, MS

ROCKRIDGE
PRESS

For general information on our other products and services or to obtain technical support, please contact our Customer Care Department within the United States at (866) 744-2665, or outside the United States at (510) 253-0500.

Rockridge Press publishes its books in a variety of electronic and print formats. Some content that appears in print may not be available in electronic books, and vice versa.

Interior and Cover Designer: Sean Doyle
Art Producer: Janice Ackerman
Editor: Anne Lowrey
Production Editor: Rachel Taenzler
Production Manager: Riley Hoffman

Photography: © Nadine Greeff, ii, 110; © Hélène Dujardin, vi, x; © Laura Flippen, Cover, p. 26; © Nataša Mandić/Stocksy, p. 42; © Rua Castilho/StockFood, p. 58; © Andrew Purcell, p. 84; © Cameron Whitman, p. 98. Illustration: © Charlie Layton: p. 12. Author Photo Courtesy of Bradford Rogne Photography.

Paperback ISBN: 978-1-63878-196-7
eBook ISBN: 979-8-88608-115-2
R0

I dedicate this book to all the clients I've seen in my private practice who have successfully lost weight, reversed prediabetes, and, importantly, kept the weight off using the principles and lifestyle taught in this book.

CONTENTS

INTRODUCTION

L et's be clear: People who develop type 2 diabetes pretty much always start with prediabetes. However, that does not mean that prediabetes is a guaranteed road to a type 2 diabetes diagnosis. In fact, small changes in your lifestyle can slow and even reverse prediabetes. This fact may not be comforting for those with a recent prediabetes diagnosis, and it's understandable to be a bit afraid and confused. However, as a registered dietitian with 20 years of experience helping clients establish health-altering lifestyle changes, I will guide you through your next steps.

So why did I decide to write this book? Let me answer that question with a story about my client Wendy. Most clients come to me for weight loss, but others are looking for far more urgent solutions, like their longevity. Most of the time, you must gain control of the former to improve the latter. Wendy was already a diabetic upon meeting with me. However, she was experiencing a condition that many people with prediabetes experience and that can lead to diabetes: insulin resistance. We'll discuss this in more detail in later chapters, but for now, know that insulin resistance is a condition that requires nearly the same lifestyle changes as those discussed in this book to improve prediabetes. Cutting calories can be a simple way to lose weight for those without chronic conditions. However, with insulin resistance, simply cutting calories isn't going to do the trick. It requires a more specialized approach for success.

After five months of working with me virtually, Wendy achieved astounding progress in improving her health. Her progress included better control of her blood sugar, a 40-pound weight loss, and reduction in her insulin. That's because the program that I've used with my clients for over 20 years is based on the diabetes exchange system that is specially designed to help people with insulin resistance control their blood sugar. Using my expertise to help people like Wendy manage their chronic diseases through nutrition and other lifestyle changes so they can live longer, happier, and healthier lives is the most rewarding part of my work. And I want to share that impact with people like you.

In this book, you'll find out everything you need to know about what changes to make to manage or reverse prediabetes as well as just how to make those changes. Nutrition-wise, you will find a host of mouthwatering but nutritious recipes customized for those with prediabetes. Although nutrition is a big part of both the risk factors for prediabetes and the remedy for potentially reversing it, nutrition is just one of many lifestyle changes you will need to confront. Weight loss is probably the number one factor in controlling blood sugar, especially when this weight is lost from your waist. A structured, consistent exercise plan can go a long way in supporting not only your weight loss efforts but also your heart health. Heart health may not seem relevant, but you should know that having insulin resistance along with an unhealthy heart can significantly increase your risk of heart disease. Finally, lowering your stress levels and improving your sleep also play a role in improving your health. You'll find guidelines on the correct way to tackle all of these and more in this book.

I wish you well on your journey to health, happiness, and longevity. Let's get started.

CHAPTER 1

Prediabetes and Weight Loss

This chapter will cover what prediabetes is, how it behaves in the body, how to measure and diagnose it, and what to do about it. You will also discover what factors put you at risk for the condition, those that are both in and out of your control. Finally, you will learn how nutrition factors into prediabetes management and reversal and get a peek at your sample meal plans.

What Prediabetes Means

Prediabetes is what it sounds like: before diabetes. It means your body is at high risk for developing type 2 diabetes if your diet and lifestyle continue the way they have been. The major defining characteristic of prediabetes is insulin resistance. Once you understand insulin resistance, you can understand prediabetes and know how to reverse it before it becomes chronic.

Many people associate the word *insulin* with diabetes, but you don't have to have diabetes or even prediabetes to have insulin resistance. Insulin is a hormone that stores blood glucose (or blood sugar) for energy. However, contrary to popular belief, insulin isn't only released when you eat carbohydrates; it's also released when you eat protein and fat.

Insulin resistance happens when the body can't fully store the glucose from your blood for energy after you eat. Your pancreas still produces insulin, but there is resistance to this insulin, preventing glucose from entering your cells. This leads to glucose levels staying high in your blood for extended periods of time.

When sugar (glucose) floats around in your blood for too long, it can weaken your immune system and cause damage to your heart, kidneys, eyes, and nerves. It also ends up being stored as fat because your body can't use it for energy, making weight loss more difficult than if you didn't have insulin resistance. What is most frustrating is that the key to reversing insulin resistance is losing weight! Once you lose fat, especially a specific type of belly fat, your body will begin to have a normal insulin response again, improving your health and weight loss efforts. We will go over how this works later in the chapter, but know that although this sounds like a vicious, inescapable cycle, the purpose of this book is to help you break it.

TRACKING BLOOD SUGAR

The primary way your doctor diagnoses prediabetes is by checking your blood sugar levels. The hallmark of diagnostics is your hemoglobin A1c, which is a number that measures how much sugar is sticking to your red blood cells.

There will still be sugar attached to the red blood cells in a body with a normal insulin response and normal blood sugar levels, but not as much as for those with prediabetes or diabetes. A measure of 5.7 percent or less is considered a normal A1c reading, meaning your insulin is acting the way it should. However, in those with prediabetes and diabetes, there is much more sugar floating around in the blood, meaning more is attaching to your red blood cells than should be.

If your A1c is between 5.7 percent and 6.4 percent, you are considered to have prediabetes. However, if it is 6.5 percent or above, your doctor will diagnose you with diabetes. Please know that the life cycle of a red blood cell is three months. Therefore, it is not helpful or an accurate result if you get an A1c test more than once in three months; otherwise, you are getting results from old cells.

There are ways for you to track your blood sugar at home to see how well it's being managed. The following table can help you.

	BLOOD SUGAR RANGE (MG/DL)
NORMAL	80 to 99
PREDIABETIC	100 to 124
DIABETIC	125+

Risk Factors

Certain factors predispose individuals to insulin resistance and prediabetes. Some of these factors can be altered, but some are out of your control. Fortunately, changing the factors that are in your hands can be enough to change your condition.

Factors beyond Your Control

It's important to recognize that some factors in prediabetes are beyond your control. Here are some important ones to note.

AGE

According to the American Diabetes Association, if you are 45 or older, your risk of diabetes and prediabetes goes up. This is simply due to increased insulin resistance that comes with an aging pancreas. As you age, your pancreas also does, which impairs its ability to produce insulin as efficiently.

GENETICS

Although experts agree there is no clear reason, some minority ethnic groups tend to have a higher risk of developing diabetes than Caucasians do. Theories such as African Americans producing less potassium and potassium deficiency being a risk factor for insulin resistance have been posited. Definitive public health statistics have shown that genetics can be a risk factor, including family history and ethnicity.

HISTORY OF GESTATIONAL DIABETES OR POLYCYSTIC OVARY SYNDROME (PCOS)

Statistically, if you developed diabetes during pregnancy (gestational diabetes), then you are likely to develop prediabetes or diabetes again later in life, especially if pregnancy weight is not lost and diet quality is poor. Polycystic ovary syndrome (PCOS) is an incurable disease that alters female hormones, making it very difficult to lose weight. This weight gain can lead to insulin resistance and, thus, prediabetes.

Factors within Your Control

Although you can't totally control these factors, you have a lot of say in how they can affect your health. Here are some alterable risk factors of developing prediabetes.

WAIST CIRCUMFERENCE

A high waist circumference is indicative of abdominal obesity, meaning an excess of visceral fat. A large amount of visceral fat is the primary culprit in the cause of insulin resistance and the inability to store and use glucose in the body properly.

WHAT YOU EAT

Prediabetes and diabetes development are closely associated with poor diet quality. Foods that promote inflammation can be detrimental to health. These include those with excess sodium and added sugar, and hyper-processed and fried foods. Finally, being in a calorie surplus while consuming these foods promotes fat gain that causes insulin resistance.

HOW MUCH YOU MOVE YOUR BODY

According to the Centers for Disease Control and Prevention (CDC), not getting enough physical activity increases risk due to physical activity's ability to help one control blood sugar. It can also help keep weight off when following a consistent exercise regimen.

HOW MUCH YOU SLEEP

The CDC also states that getting less than seven hours of sleep per night increases your risk of diabetes due to an increased prevalence of insulin resistance seen in those who are consistently sleep-deprived. Lack of sleep also disrupts your hunger hormones, which can cause you to overeat and promote weight gain.

SMOKING

Smokers are 30 to 40 percent more likely to develop type 2 diabetes than nonsmokers. This is because the chemicals in cigarettes may disrupt the effectiveness of insulin and can promote abdominal obesity.

The Role of Weight Loss

A recent study consistent with other diabetes research findings shows that a loss of 15 percent body weight can have a major impact on type 2 diabetes progression and even result in diabetes remission in some patients. If you have prediabetes, this means you can reverse your condition with weight loss and maintenance of that weight loss.

This is especially effective when you lose fat from your midsection. This type of fat is called *visceral fat* and is the worst type you can carry on your body. Visceral fat is inflammatory and surrounds your organs. This *deep fat* or *abdominal fat* is in an area that lies out of reach, so it cannot be easily pinched or felt, but an excess is associated with chronic diseases. If a woman has a waist circumference of more than 35 inches and a man has a circumference of more than 40 inches, their risk of chronic disease, like prediabetes and diabetes, increases dramatically. This is because this fat releases chemicals called *cytokines* that are poisonous to the body and cause damage.

Furthermore, this fat blocks the receptors in the body from accepting the glucose your insulin is attempting to store for energy. Thus, if you can reduce your waistline size with a healthier lifestyle and the type of anti-inflammatory foods found in this book's recipes, then you have a very good chance at reversing prediabetes.

Prediabetes Nutrition

There are three macronutrients that contain calories: carbohydrates, protein, and fat. Although carbohydrates elicit the most dramatic spikes in blood sugar (and, thus, insulin as a response), protein and fat contribute to this process as well. What's more, the entire diet plays a role in either improving or worsening one's health, regardless of the carbohydrate content. Even if you cut out carbohydrates and your diet quality is poor, your health, weight, and blood sugar control will still suffer. In this section, we will cover how food impacts prediabetes and health so that you can make the best decisions possible.

Carbs and Sugar

Out of the macronutrients, carbohydrates are the most responsible for energy. This is because carbohydrates contain glucose, which is the brain's preferred source of fuel and a source of energy for the rest of your body. Glucose in the blood is also called *blood sugar*, which is why carbohydrates have the biggest impact on blood sugar levels. When you eat carbs, the body breaks them down into glucose, which, upon entering your bloodstream, tells your brain to release insulin. It is insulin's job to shuttle this glucose to the brain, muscles, organs, and other tissues to use for energy. Any extra glucose is stored for later use in the liver and muscles as "glycogen," and when glycogen stores are full, glucose is stored as fat.

Now, it's important to note that blood sugar spikes and insulin release are a normal, healthy part of metabolism. However, in those with type 2 diabetes, this system does not work effectively. Not enough insulin is released to put away the glucose the way it should, so glucose hangs around in the blood, keeping blood sugar levels high. This is dangerous for the body. Those with prediabetes and insulin resistance experience the same effect, but to a lesser extent.

Blood sugar spikes can be harmful to those with impaired insulin function. One thing that helps mitigate this is consuming carbohydrates high in fiber. That's because fiber breaks down slowly in the stomach, thus slowing digestion and creating lower blood sugar levels. On the other end of this spectrum, food high in added sugars causes a more dramatic spike in blood sugar due to its rapid digestion and absorption into your system. Look under the Total Carbohydrates section of the nutritional label for fiber and added sugar content when reading food labels. Fiber is always listed, and added sugar is found on some labels, but it is becoming common under the carbohydrates section.

It's important to know there is no set amount of carbohydrates for one to consume. The recommended daily servings of carbohydrates are individualized based on weight, height, activity level, and lifestyle. Speak to a registered dietitian to inform yourself on the specific amounts for you.

SMART CARBOHYDRATE CHOICES FOR PREDIABETES:

- Brown and black rice

- Farro

- Fruits

- Oats

- Quinoa

- Vegetables (including beans, lentils, and potatoes)

- Whole-grain bread and pasta

Protein

Protein is a macronutrient found in both animal and plant food sources. Contrary to popular belief, protein doesn't only play a role in gaining muscle but is also vital to many bodily functions. We need protein for healthy skin, hair, and nails, to produce enzymes and hormones, make antibodies for our immune system, and build and heal body tissues after injury. Protein is also a source of energy and can cause a rise in blood sugar but with a milder response than carbohydrates.

Protein is also the most satiating of the macronutrients. This is because protein molecules take longer to break down in the stomach. When compared to carbs and fat, protein makes us feel the most satisfied after a meal and keeps us feeling this way longer. I recommend that protein be included in every meal and snack for my clients. Eating sufficient protein also helps to prevent overeating.

In the context of blood sugar control, it is even more important for those with insulin resistance to include protein in their meals to control blood sugar spikes. Preventing overeating is also important for controlling the weight gain that can exacerbate insulin resistance. Including 15 to 20 grams of protein in each meal is the standard recommendation.

SMART PROTEIN CHOICES FOR PREDIABETES:

- Dairy

- Eggs

- Lean meats

- Poultry

- Seafood

- Soy and legumes

Fat

Fat has gone through reputation ebbs and flows and recently surged in popularity. I'm here to tell you that fat has a place in your diet regardless of your health state. Fats are essential for health and are responsible for some major body functions. We need fats to produce hormones such as testosterone and estrogen. This is why when some women are in a calorie deficit for an extended period and they aren't consuming enough fat, they may have a disrupted menstrual cycle (which is unhealthy for the body).

Fats are also responsible for storing the fat-soluble vitamins—A, D, E, and K. The brain is also 60 percent fat, and we need fats from our diet for optimal brain function. Omega-3 fatty acids are a type of fat vital for brain function and fighting inflammation. These fats are of notable importance to those with insulin resistance and diabetes. Not only are omega-3s essential, meaning we must get them from our diet and cannot make them on our own, they play a vital role in heart health and inflammation. Those with insulin resistance are at higher risk of heart disease due to damage to the cardio-vascular system with consistently high blood sugar.

Additionally, to lose the visceral fat that causes insulin resistance, one must adhere to an anti-inflammatory diet, and omega-3s are a strong source of anti-inflammatory compounds along with other types of unsaturated fats. Saturated and trans fats should be consumed sparingly, as they have adverse health effects in excess. Take note that fats are the most calorie-dense of the macronutrients (9 calories per gram compared to only 4 calories per gram of protein and carbs), so you should consume even unsaturated fats with care.

SMART FAT CHOICES FOR PREDIABETES:

- Avocados
- Cooking oils (canola, olive, etc.)
- Nut butters (peanut, almond, etc.)
- Nuts and seeds
- Olives
- Salmon and other fatty fish

Other Essential Nutrients

Now that we've covered the macronutrients, there are other nutrients to note that also play a role in managing prediabetes and insulin resistance.

FIBER

Fiber is a type of carbohydrate that does not contain calories and provides structure to food. There are three types of fiber: soluble, insoluble, and fermentable (or prebiotic). All three are beneficial to the body in their own way. Soluble fiber, found in oats, beans, and other vegetables, absorbs cholesterol in the intestines and works to excrete it from the body, improving heart health. It also slows the absorption of sugar in the bloodstream by slowing digestion. Insoluble fiber, found in whole grains and produce, cannot be broken down by digestive chemicals and, thus, acts as a scrub brush for the intestines, assisting digestion. Prebiotic fiber feeds the good bacteria, known as *probiotics*, in our gut, which can help keep the gut healthy. A healthy gut can help with blood sugar control.

POTASSIUM

Potassium has an antagonistic effect on sodium in the body. Both are electrolytes that aid in hydration and muscle function, but potassium promotes healthier blood flow, lower blood pressure, and bone health. Individuals who consume enough potassium tend to have better blood sugar control, mainly because fruits and vegetables are high in potassium.

SODIUM

Sodium is an electrolyte we need for bodily functions such as muscle contraction and maintaining hydration status. However, sodium has been known to raise blood pressure and be harmful to heart health in excess.

CREATING A BALANCED MEAL

When eating for prediabetes, balancing macronutrients for optimal blood sugar control is essential. If you were to eat a meal composed of all—or mainly—carbohydrates, your blood sugar would spike dramatically, which is not something you want. However, blood sugar is not the only factor. Meals composed primarily of protein and fat will leave you with low energy, which is why you need carbs, even with insulin resistance. The key is to have the correct balance of these macronutrients in your meal, and to do that, you must know how to build your plate. I will be providing meal plans using the recipes in this book, but you should keep these guidelines in mind when you eat outside the plan, such as when you are out at restaurants, at family gatherings, or having similar meals. Remember these guidelines:

1. Learn how to design your plate: Half the plate should be a colorful mix of non-starchy vegetables, such as broccoli, cauliflower, carrots, Brussels sprouts, asparagus, and green leafy vegetables. One quarter should be a superfood carbs such as quinoa, sweet potatoes, purple potatoes, beans, lentils, brown rice, and black rice. The last quarter should be a lean protein, such as chicken, salmon, sirloin steak, tofu, or tempeh.

2. Have the right-size plate. Studies have shown that the larger the plate, the more food you will pile on it. Plates 8 to 9 inches in diameter will help you visualize the plate quadrants and make you feel like your plate is full.

3. Use measuring cups. Using these tools allows you to know exactly how much you are serving yourself at each meal.

It is useful to look at some examples of how my meal plans are structured to keep a balanced meal. The first example combines three different recipes to reflect my guidelines. However, the second example is a recipe that is already balanced when you combine all the ingredients. In the third example, the recipe contains good portions of protein and vegetables but needs a supplement of healthy carbohydrates.

Example 1: ½ plate Sheet Pan Roasted Vegetables (see page 100) plus ¼ plate Baked Salmon with Balsamic Glaze (see page 105) plus ¼ plate Black Forbidden Rice with Bell Peppers (see page 107)

Example 2: Fried Farro with Shrimp and Veggies (see page 73)

Example 3: Primavera Frittata (see page 50) plus 1 cup fruit of choice

Determining Caloric Intake and Food Servings

Knowing what to eat is only half the battle in improving health. Knowing *how much* to eat is also a key component you cannot ignore. Eating too many (or too few) calories has a significant impact not only on weight but also on consistent blood glucose readings. Additionally, there is such a thing as overeating healthy food—even if your intentions are good. So, in this section, we'll go over guidelines about calories and portions to keep in mind as you proceed on your journey to managing insulin resistance.

Daily Caloric Intake

Although specific calorie goals vary from person to person, everyone should follow core eating principles to control weight and support health. Especially where blood sugar control is concerned, eating frequency is crucial. Skipping meals can disrupt your hunger hormones and cause you to overeat later in the day. A big compensation meal will exacerbate insulin resistance.

A larger amount of food eaten in one sitting causes a more dramatic spike in blood sugar, which is tougher for your body to control without normal insulin function. That's why I recommend eating a meal or snack every 3 to 4 hours, for both consistent blood sugar patterns and hunger control. Additionally, eating a meal containing only (or primarily) carbohydrates will produce a larger spike in insulin than a balanced meal containing a blend of carbs, protein, and fat. For weight loss to occur, we need to consume fewer calories than we burn. Following the plan in this book using the recipes developed specifically for healthy blood sugar control will help you control your weight and, thus, insulin resistance.

PORTION CONTROL

Regardless of whether your goal is to manage prediabetes or maintain weight/prevent weight gain, you should always be mindful of your food portions. Even if you are mindfully eating all the recommended nutritious foods, it's still important to pay attention to your portion sizes. You could applaud yourself for eating avocado toast with an egg on whole-grain bread, but if you're overeating this nutritious food, you'll find weight loss difficult due to a calorie surplus. In other words, you could be eating more calories than you are burning, making it nearly impossible to see weight loss.

Specific portions will vary depending on certain factors such as your weight, activity level, and gender. However, I tell my clients to "talk to your hand" to figure out portion sizes as a rule of thumb. Use your hand as a measuring tool when eating meals outside the recipes provided in this book.

Fist (1 cup): Use your fist to judge two servings of cooked pasta, rice, or other grain.

Palm (3 ounces to 6 ounces): Use your palm to judge the size of the meat. Small palms measure about 3 to 4 ounces and bigger palms about 5 to 6 ounces.

Thumb (1 teaspoon): Use the tip of your thumb to measure a pat of butter. Use the length from the knuckle of your thumb to its tip to judge a serving of salad dressing (1 tablespoon).

Remember, eating meals that are too large could promote an unfavorable increase in blood sugar and possibly a surplus of calories. That's why the meal plan provided in this book is calculated carefully and portioned to keep you on the right track.

Foods to Enjoy, Avoid, and Eat in Moderation

This section is not intended to label certain foods as "good" or "bad." There are simply some foods that promote health and blood sugar control better than others. Even the "enjoy freely" foods should be eaten with a certain amount of precision so you don't exceed the calorie goal set to maintain or promote weight loss. The "foods to limit" are usually from sources that do not align with the health goals in this book, and they tend to be calorie-dense and higher in saturated fat, trans fats, and sodium.

Foods to Enjoy Freely

- Eggs
- Fermented dairy (Greek yogurt, kefir, etc.)
- Fermented vegetables
- Fruits and vegetables
- Lean meats (poultry, seafood, lean cuts of beef and pork)
- Milk (of choice)
- Whole grains (whole-wheat bread/pasta, brown rice)

Foods to Eat in Moderation

- Condiments such as mayo, ketchup, and salad dressing
- Dark chocolate (70 percent or higher)
- Moderately fatty meats, fatty cuts of beef and pork, dark-meat chicken
- Nuts and seeds
- Oils

Foods to Limit

- Candy
- Desserts (cookies, cakes, pastries)
- Fast food (hamburgers, pizza, fries)
- High-fat meats (bacon, cured meats, etc.)
- Ice cream
- Potato chips and similar snacks

14-Day Weight Loss Meal Plan

This weight loss plan is one you don't have to dread for fear of being boring or difficult. I have crafted this plan based on my years of experience in helping clients lose weight and customized it to an individual with prediabetes. It includes recipes for your daily main meals, snacks, and exercise routines. The recipes include tips to make cooking easier, reduce food waste, and guide you through hassle-free meal prep and planning.

Here's what you can expect from this meal plan:

- Serves one person and makes smart use of leftovers.

- All the ingredients are easy to find and will be reused across recipes to reduce food waste and overspending at the grocery store.

- Considers the proportions of carbs, protein, and fat for insulin resistance management. These meals maintain balance by being low to moderate in carbohydrates, high in protein, and moderate in fat.

- Includes an average of 1,500 calories depending on your individual needs. This means that some days might be 1,350 calories and other days 1,600 calories, so don't be alarmed. At the end of the week, your daily calorie goal will average out to 1,500, and each day will be labeled for you.

- Note that exercise will alter your calorie needs slightly in the following ways:

  - If you are a female and exercise fewer than three days, follow 1,300 calories.

  - If you are a female and exercise for three days, follow 1,500 calories.

  - If you are a female and exercise for more than three days, follow 1,700 calories.

  - If you are a male and exercise for three days, follow 1,800 calories.

  - If you are a male and exercise for more than three days, follow 2,100 calories.

- Exercise should be done no more than five times a week. If you follow the preceding calorie recommendations pertaining to exercise and are not losing weight, do not increase your exercise but lower your calorie needs by 200 calories per day.

- If you need to bump up your calories, add an extra snack or dessert. If you need to bulk up your meals as a male, double the portion of one of your meals, double one of the snacks, or add a second snack to your day. Everything is labeled for you, so all you have to do is a quick calculation to determine your calorie goal.

You can always double your sides, double the snack portions, or add a dessert if you need more calories.

- Conversely, if you need to lower your calorie intake, you have the option to remove the snacks.

Week 1 Meal Plan

	Breakfast	Lunch	Dinner	Snacks	Total Calories
MONDAY	Canadian Bacon, Spinach, and Cheese Quiches (page 51) Calories: 209 1 cup of blueberries Calories: 60	Latino Mediterranean Salad (page 61) Calories: 318 Greek-Inspired Roasted Chicken Breast (see page 104) Calories: 159	Roasted Eggplant, Butternut Squash, and Sirloin Steak Stew (page 64) Calories: 390 ½ ounce 75 percent dark chocolate Calories: 80	Cottage Cheese Parfait (page 91) Calories: 228	**1,444**
TUESDAY	Mixed Berry Yogurt Smoothie (page 45) Calories: 358	Blackened Salmon (page 74) Calories: 243 Black Forbidden Rice with Bell Peppers (page 107) Calories: 196 Steamed Broccoli and Cauliflower with Lemon (page 102) Calories: 76	Fried Farro with Shrimp and Veggies (page 73) Calories: 435	Low-Carb Quesadilla (page 86) Calories: 214	**1,522**

	Breakfast	Lunch	Dinner	Snacks	Total Calories
WEDNESDAY	*Leftover: Canadian Bacon, Spinach, and Cheese Quiches* Calories: 209 1 cup of blueberries Calories: 60	*Leftover: Latino Mediterranean Salad* Calories: 318 *Leftover: Greek-Inspired Roasted Chicken Breast* Calories: 159	*Leftover: Roasted Eggplant, Butternut Squash, and Sirloin Steak Stew* Calories: 390 ½ ounce 75 percent dark chocolate Calories: 80	Cottage Cheese Parfait (page 91) Calories: 228	**1,444**
THURSDAY	Mixed Berry Yogurt Smoothie (page 45) Calories: 358	*Leftover: Blackened Salmon* Calories: 243 *Leftover: Black Forbidden Rice with Bell Peppers* Calories: 196 *Leftover: Steamed Broccoli and Cauliflower with Lemon* Calories: 76	*Leftover: Fried Farro with Shrimp and Veggies* Calories: 435	Low-Carb Quesadilla (page 86) Calories: 214	**1,522**

	Breakfast	Lunch	Dinner	Snacks	Total Calories
FRIDAY	*Leftover: Canadian Bacon, Spinach, and Cheese Quiches* Calories: 209 1 cup of blueberries Calories: 60	*Leftover: Latino Mediterranean Salad* Calories: 318 *Leftover: Greek-Inspired Roasted Chicken Breast* Calories: 159	*Leftover: Roasted Eggplant, Butternut Squash, and Sirloin Steak Stew* Calories: 390 ½ ounce 75 percent dark chocolate Calories: 80	Roast Beef and Vegetable Rolls (page 89) Calories: 132 Apple-Pineapple Bake (page 95) Calories: 257	**1,605**
SATURDAY	Oat-Apple Spiced Smoothie (page 47) Calories: 217	*Leftover: Blackened Salmon* Calories: 243 *Leftover: Black Forbidden Rice with Bell Peppers* Calories: 196 *Leftover: Steamed Broccoli and Cauliflower with Lemon* Calories: 76	*Leftover: Fried Farro with Shrimp and Veggies* Calories: 435 High-Protein Mango Mousse (page 94) Calories: 147	*Leftover: Roast Beef and Vegetable Rolls* Calories: 132	**1,446**

	Breakfast	Lunch	Dinner	Snacks	Total Calories
SUNDAY	Leftover: Canadian Bacon, Spinach, and Cheese Quiches Calories: 209 1 cup of blueberries Calories: 60	Leftover: Latino Mediterranean Salad Calories: 318 Leftover: Greek-Inspired Roasted Chicken Breast Calories: 159	Leftover: Roasted Eggplant, Butternut Squash, and Sirloin Steak Stew Calories: 390 ½ ounce 75 percent dark chocolate Calories: 80	Leftover: Roast Beef and Vegetable Rolls Calories: 132 Leftover: Apple-Pineapple Bake Calories: 257	1,605

Week 1 Shopping List

CANNED AND BOTTLED ITEMS

☐ Applesauce, unsweetened (¼ cup)

☐ Balsamic glaze, 1 (8-ounce) bottle

☐ Broth, chicken or vegetable, low-sodium, 2 (32-ounce) cartons

☐ Garlic, minced, 1 (8-ounce) jar

☐ Ginger, crushed, 1 (4-ounce) bottle

☐ Honey, 1 (8-ounce) bottle or jar

☐ Nonstick cooking spray, 1 bottle

☐ Oil, olive, extra-virgin, 1 (16-ounce) bottle

☐ Oil, sesame, 1 (12-ounce) bottle

☐ Olives, kalamata, pitted (½ cup)

☐ Pineapple chunks in 100 percent pineapple juice, 1 cup

☐ Protein powder, vanilla (whey, soy, or pea), 1 container

☐ Soy sauce, low-sodium, 1 bottle

☐ Tomatoes, diced, low-sodium, 2 (15½-ounce) cans

☐ Vanilla extract, pure, 1 small bottle

EGGS AND DAIRY

☐ Butter, light (¼ cup)

☐ Cheese, cottage, 2 percent cultured small curds (1 cup)

☐ Cheese, mozzarella, shredded part-skim (7 ounces)

☐ Cheese, queso fresco (10 ounces)

- [ ] Eggs, large (12)
- [ ] Egg whites, 1½ cups
- [ ] Milk, 1 percent (2⅛ cups)
- [ ] Oat beverage, low-fat, 1 (2-pound) container
- [ ] Yogurt, Greek, 2 percent plain (1½ cups)

MEAT, POULTRY, AND SEAFOOD

- [ ] Bacon, Canadian (3 ounces)
- [ ] Beef, roast, deli slices (8 ounces)
- [ ] Beef, top sirloin strip steak (2 pounds)
- [ ] Chicken, breasts, boneless, skinless (1 pound)
- [ ] Salmon, fillets, skin-on (20 ounces)
- [ ] Shrimp, large (20/25 count), peeled and deveined (2 pounds)

PANTRY ITEMS

- [ ] Cayenne pepper
- [ ] Chocolate, 75 percent dark (2 ounces)
- [ ] Cinnamon, ground
- [ ] Cloves, ground
- [ ] Cumin, ground
- [ ] Farro, 1 (8.8-ounce) bag
- [ ] Garlic powder
- [ ] Monk fruit sweetener, 1 small bag
- [ ] Nutmeg, ground
- [ ] Oats, quick, 1 (18-ounce) container
- [ ] Oregano, dried
- [ ] Paprika, smoked
- [ ] Pecans, pieces, 1 (8-ounce) bag
- [ ] Pepper, black, freshly ground
- [ ] Rice, black (2 cups)
- [ ] Salt, sea
- [ ] Thyme, dried
- [ ] Tortillas, 8-inch low-carb (1 pack)
- [ ] Walnuts, crushed, 1 small bag

PRODUCE

- [ ] Apples, Honeycrisp (1 pound)
- [ ] Avocado (1)
- [ ] Basil (1 bunch)
- [ ] Bell pepper, red (2)
- [ ] Blueberries (4 cups)
- [ ] Broccoli (1 head)

- ☐ Butternut squash (1)
- ☐ Carrots (2)
- ☐ Cauliflower (1 head)
- ☐ Celery (8 stalks)
- ☐ Cucumber, Persian (2)
- ☐ Eggplant (1)
- ☐ Lemons (4)

- ☐ Mushrooms (6 ounces)
- ☐ Onion, red (2)
- ☐ Onion, yellow (2)
- ☐ Scallions (8)
- ☐ Tomatoes, cherry (1 cup)
- ☐ Zucchini (1)

FROZEN

- ☐ Berries (3½ cups)
- ☐ Mango (1 cup)
- ☐ Peas (1 cup)

- ☐ Spinach (3 cups)
- ☐ Vegetables, mixed (corn, peas, green beans, and carrots) (6 cups)

Week 1 Prep Ahead

- Prep the Flavorful Farro (page 108) ahead of time. You'll use it in the Fried Farro with Shrimp and Veggies.

- Prep the smoothies and parfaits to store in jars to save cooking time throughout the week.

- Chop your basil leaves to store, refrigerated, in a container, as you'll use them for the Latino Mediterranean Salad.

- The leftover recipes are based on what would be left over for one person. Make more ahead of time if you are cooking for people other than yourself for this meal plan.

Week 2 Meal Plan

	Breakfast	Lunch	Dinner	Snacks	Total Calories
MONDAY	Pumpkin–Greek Yogurt Overnight Oats (page 53) Calories: 300	Spicy Beef Burgers (page 68) Calories: 156 Butternut Squash, Carrot, and Sweet Potato Fries (page 101) Calories: 82	Mediterranean Chicken with Artichokes and Olives (page 75) Calories: 330 Flavorful Farro (page 108) Calories: 92	Blueberry High-Fiber Muffins (page 56) Calories: 192 1 cup 1 percent milk Calories: 100	**1,252**
TUESDAY	Mango-Avocado-Spinach Smoothie (page 44) Calories: 450	Soy-Ginger Pork Tenderloin (page 66) Calories: 346 Black Forbidden Rice with Bell Peppers (page 107) Calories: 196	High-Protein Spaghetti with Creamy Butternut Squash Sauce (page 76) Calories: 380 Greek-Inspired Roasted Chicken Breast (see page 104) Calories: 159	Low-Carb Quesadilla (page 86) Calories: 214	**1,745**
WEDNESDAY	*Leftover: Pumpkin–Greek Yogurt Overnight Oats* Calories: 300	*Leftover: Spicy Beef Burgers* Calories: 156 *Leftover: Butternut Squash, Carrot, and Sweet Potato Fries* Calories: 82	*Leftover: Mediterranean Chicken with Artichokes and Olives* Calories: 330 *Leftover: Flavorful Farro* Calories: 92	*Leftover: Blueberry High-Fiber Muffins* Calories: 192 1 cup 1 percent milk Calories: 100	**1,252**

	Breakfast	Lunch	Dinner	Snacks	Total Calories
THURSDAY	Mango-Avocado-Spinach Smoothie (page 44) Calories: 450	*Leftover: Soy-Ginger Pork Tenderloin* Calories: 346 *Leftover: Black Forbidden Rice with Bell Peppers* Calories: 196	*Leftover: High-Protein Spaghetti with Creamy Butternut Squash Sauce* Calories: 380 *Leftover: Greek-Inspired Roasted Chicken Breast* Calories: 159	Low-Carb Quesadilla (page 86) Calories: 214	**1,745**
FRIDAY	*Leftover: Pumpkin–Greek Yogurt Overnight Oats* Calories: 300	*Leftover: Spicy Beef Burgers* Calories: 156 *Leftover: Butternut Squash, Carrot, and Sweet Potato Fries* Calories: 82	*Leftover: Mediterranean Chicken with Artichokes and Olives* Calories: 330 *Leftover: Flavorful Farro* Calories: 92	*Leftover: Blueberry High-Fiber Muffins* Calories: 192 1 cup 1 percent milk Calories: 100	**1,252**

	Breakfast	Lunch	Dinner	Snacks	Total Calories
SATURDAY	Queso Fresco, Tomato, and Avocado Wrap (page 49) Calories: 522	*Leftover: Soy-Ginger Pork Tenderloin* Calories: 346 *Leftover: Black Forbidden Rice with Bell Peppers* Calories: 196	*Leftover: High-Protein Spaghetti with Creamy Butternut Squash Sauce* Calories: 380 *Leftover: Greek-Inspired Roasted Chicken Breast* Calories: 159	*Leftover: Blueberry High-Fiber Muffins* Calories: 192 1 cup 1 percent milk Calories: 100	**1,895**
SUNDAY	*Leftover: Pumpkin–Greek Yogurt Overnight Oats* Calories: 300	*Leftover: Spicy Beef Burgers* Calories: 156 *Leftover: Butternut Squash, Carrot, and Sweet Potato Fries* Calories: 82	*Leftover: Mediterranean Chicken with Artichokes and Olives* Calories: 330 *Leftover: Flavorful Farro* Calories: 92	*Leftover: Blueberry High-Fiber Muffins* Calories: 192 1 cup 1 percent milk Calories: 100	**1,252**

Week 2 Shopping List

CANNED AND BOTTLED ITEMS

- ☐ Artichoke hearts, 2 (14-ounce) cans
- ☐ Broth, chicken or vegetable, low-sodium, 2 (32-ounce) cartons
- ☐ Mayonnaise dressing, olive oil, 1 (8-ounce) jar
- ☐ Oil, canola, 1 (16-ounce) bottle

- ☐ Olives, kalamata, pitted and halved (¾ cup)
- ☐ Pineapple, crushed, canned (½ cup)
- ☐ Pineapple, diced in 100 percent juice (½ cup)
- ☐ Pumpkin puree (1 cup)

EGGS AND DAIRY

- ☐ Cheese, cheddar, sharp (1 cup)
- ☐ Cheese, cottage, low-fat (1 cup)
- ☐ Cheese, mozzarella, part-skim shredded (4 ounces)
- ☐ Cheese, parmesan, shredded (1 cup)
- ☐ Cheese, queso fresco (2 ounces)

- ☐ Eggs, large (2)
- ☐ Milk, 1 percent (11 cups)
- ☐ Milk, 2 percent (¾ cup)
- ☐ Yogurt, Greek, 2 percent, plain (3 cups)

MEAT, POULTRY, AND SEAFOOD

- ☐ Beef, ground, lean (1 pound)
- ☐ Chicken breasts, boneless, skinless (2 pounds)

- ☐ Chicken, breast tenders, unbreaded (1 pound)
- ☐ Pork tenderloin (1½ pounds)

PANTRY ITEMS

- ☐ Baking powder
- ☐ Baking soda
- ☐ Chia seeds, 1 small bag
- ☐ Cornstarch

- ☐ Flour, all-purpose (1 cup)
- ☐ Lavash bread, whole-grain, 1 (10-by-8-inch) loaf
- ☐ Psyllium husk (1¼ cups)

- [ ] Rice, black (2 cups)
- [ ] Rolled oats (1 cup)
- [ ] Sesame seeds (2 tablespoons)
- [ ] Spaghetti, high-fiber protein (8 ounces)
- [ ] Tortilla, 8-inch, low-carb (3)

PRODUCE

- [ ] Arugula, 1 (10-ounce) bag
- [ ] Avocados (2)
- [ ] Basil (1 bunch)
- [ ] Bell pepper, red (2)
- [ ] Blueberries (2 cups)
- [ ] Butternut squash (1)
- [ ] Carrots (2)
- [ ] Cilantro (1 bunch)
- [ ] Limes (4)
- [ ] Onion, red (4)
- [ ] Onion, yellow onion (2)
- [ ] Pepper, jalapeño (1)
- [ ] Spinach, baby (12 cups)
- [ ] Sweet potato (1)
- [ ] Tomato (1)

FROZEN

- [ ] Broccoli florets (2 cups)
- [ ] Green beans (1 pound)
- [ ] Mango (½ cup)

⬆ Blackened Salmon (page 74); Flavorful Farro (page 108);
Sheet Pan Roasted Vegetables (page 100)

CHAPTER 2

Beyond Diet: Goals, Exercise, Meal Planning

Diet is likely the most important part of your journey to control prediabetes and insulin resistance. However, there are other vital factors to consider. In this section, we'll talk about how to set yourself up for success to meet your goals, the role of exercise and other factors that affect weight, and more.

Setting Weight Loss Goals

Whenever you set a goal that you cannot meet, you are not setting yourself up for success. The number one reason to miss a goal is it is either too broad or unrealistic. For example, the goal "I want to lose a lot of weight" is too broad, and without a plan, you'll probably end up frustrated and feeling defeated. This is why it is important to make goals SMART (specific, measurable, attainable, relevant, time-bound) to meet your health and weight loss goals.

Let's take "I want to lose a lot of weight" and turn it into a SMART goal:

- Specific: How much weight do you want to lose? Put a specific number on it. If you want to lose 15 pounds, that is specific and clear.

- Measurable: What's your plan to track your progress? Daily weigh-ins are not recommended because your weight fluctuates day to day. Tell yourself you will weigh yourself once a week to see how you are doing.

- Attainable: Make sure your goal and timeline to accomplish it are within your reach. For example, if you want to lose 50 pounds, start with 15 first. It'll be much easier and faster for you to achieve this goal, and once you do, you'll have the confidence to keep going until you've lost 50 pounds.

- Relevant: What does your goal mean to you? For example, if your doctor told you that your heart health is in danger, that's a powerful motivator as you work toward your goal.

- Time-bound: What's your time limit? Trying to lose 15 pounds over six months isn't an effective goal. Give yourself a realistic time limit, such as eight weeks, to achieve this goal so you don't end up disappointed.

Please note that if you have underlying health conditions such as a personal or family history of disordered eating, are pregnant, or are experiencing any other similar health condition, you should always consult with your doctor before starting any new diet or exercise regimen.

Finally, know that even with a good set of realistic goals, you must also adopt mindful habits to see weight loss. These include taking time out for food shopping, making it to the gym, meal prepping, and meal planning. The good news is this book will help make all this less overwhelming because it will provide you with delicious recipes, shopping lists, and meal plans.

Exercise

The American Diabetes Association recommends regular exercise as a part of any plan to manage insulin resistance due to exercise's ability to make your cells more sensitive to insulin. This sensitivity combats insulin resistance because it can make your insulin more effective. In this section, we'll talk about different types of exercise effective for weight loss and give some examples of common movements you can incorporate.

Cardiovascular Exercise (Cardio)

The type of exercises recommended in this section are a "HIIT" in the fitness world. High-intensity interval training (HIIT) is the most effective type of cardio for losing fat, which is crucial if we want to improve insulin resistance. What makes HIIT different from other types of cardio is that it helps you burn fat while also preserving your muscle. Therefore, 20 to 30 minutes of HIIT a minimum of two times a week is a strong recommendation for losing fat while preserving your muscle, contrary to exercises using the treadmill or elliptical.

EXAMPLE 1: BURPEES
Targets the quads, glutes, and shoulders

- Stand with your feet shoulder-width apart. Keep your weight on your heels.

- Sit your hips back and bend your knees into a squat.

- Place your hands on the floor directly in front of and just inside your feet. Now shift your weight onto your hands.

- Jump your feet back to land (softly!) on the balls of your feet in a plank position.

- Be careful not to let your back sag or your butt stick up in the air to keep the core engaged.

- Jump your feet back up so that they land just outside your hands in the position you started in.

- Stand up and reach your arms overhead.

- Push off your heels to explosively jump high into the air.

- Land and immediately sit back to start again.

- Do this 10 times as a set and perform three sets with one minute of rest in between.

Targets the upper and lower abs

- Start in a plank position. Keep your back flat and your butt down with a neutral spine.

- Engage your core and use those muscles to pull in your right knee, bringing it toward your elbow.

- Return the right knee to the starting position as you simultaneously pull your left knee in toward your left elbow. Return to the starting position.

- Continue switching legs and begin to pick up the pace until it feels like you're running in place in a plank position.

- Don't just throw your legs around. Consciously flex your core to pull your knees in.

- Continue "running" for 30 seconds for a set. Perform four sets.

EXAMPLE 3: JUMP SQUATS
Targets the quads and glutes

- Stand with your feet shoulder-width apart.

- Start by doing a regular squat (instructions in next section) and jump up explosively, pushing up from your heels.

- Land softly; then lower your body back into the squat position to complete one rep. Make sure you land with your entire foot on the ground. Repeat.

- Do this 15 times for a set. Perform three sets.

Strength Training

Contrary to popular belief, strength training is not just for getting bigger muscles. It may not pack the heart-healthy benefits of cardio, but it makes you stronger and helps you burn more calories post-exercise from lifting weights. It is also just as important for glucose control in terms of conditioning the body. You should do strength training no more than 45 minutes to 1 hour per day for a minimum of three days a week.

EXERCISE 1: SQUATS

Targets the quads and glutes

- Start with your feet hip-distance apart.

- Keeping your knees over your ankles, sit your butt back as if you're sitting down, and bend your knees. Do not arch your back and keep your spine straight all the way down.

- Keep sitting until your butt and hips are parallel to the ground. If you can go deeper without bending your spine, do so.

- Flex your butt and thighs to push your weight through your heels to raise up again.

- Do this 12 times as a set and perform three sets.

EXERCISE 2: LUNGES

Targets the quads, hamstrings, and glutes

- Keep your hands on your hips for balance.

- Step your working leg forward ahead of you with the back leg hip-distance apart until you are in a split stance like you are taking a large step. The heel of the back leg should be off the ground.

- Bend your front knee by sinking down, NOT by pushing the knee over the toes. Keep the front knee over your ankle.

- The endpoint is when the front leg makes a 90-degree angle.

- Push into your front heel to rise to your starting split stance and repeat.

- Do this 10 times on each leg as a set (20 lunges total per set) and perform three sets.

EXERCISE 3: CALF RAISES

Targets the calves

- Stand near a wall or table (so you can reach out to keep your balance); then push up onto your toes.

- Hold for two seconds; then slowly lower the heels back to the ground.

- Do the exercise on one leg or with your heels hanging off a step to make it more challenging.

- Do this 20 times with both legs (10 times on each leg if performing the single-leg variation) and perform three sets.

EXERCISE 4: PUSH-UPS
Targets the chest and front shoulders

- Start in a plank position with your arms fully extended and palms just wider than shoulder-width apart and placed just next to and outside the chest.

- Keep your neck neutral and gaze slightly forward on the ground. Do not tuck your chin.

- Press your palms into the floor and keep your feet together. Engage your thighs and core as if holding a plank to keep the lower body stiff throughout the exercise.

- Bend your elbows back at 45-degree angles to lower the entire body toward the floor. Do not let them flare out to the sides.

- Pause when your chest is barely touching the floor.

- Exhale and press into your palms to push the body away from the floor to return to the starting position.

- Do this 10 to 20 times as a set and perform three sets.

EXERCISE 5: TRICEP DIPS
Targets the triceps

- Sit with your palms on the floor behind you and at your sides and your knees bent at 90 degrees.

- Angle the direction of your palms so that your fingertips are pointing forward.

- Raise your hips off the ground into the starting position. You will only be using your arms for resistance. Do not use your hips or legs during this exercise.

- Bend your elbows back, not out to the side, and lower your body toward the ground until you feel the tension in your triceps.

- Straighten your arms to the starting position and repeat.

- To increase difficulty, straighten your legs so only the bottoms of your heels are on the ground.

- Do this 15 to 20 times as a set and perform three sets.

EXERCISE 6: BICEP CURL

Targets the biceps

- Stand with your feet shoulder-width apart, arms at your sides and palms facing forward.

- Keeping the core tight, tightly grip dumbbells, barbells, or something heavy in either hand.

- Bring your wrists toward your upper chest and stop when you feel maximum tension on the biceps.

- Squeeze the biceps at the top and hold for three seconds; then slowly bring both arms back down to the sides.

- Do this 12 times for a set and perform three sets.

EXERCISE 7: BODYWEIGHT SHOULDER PRESS

Targets the shoulders

- Position yourself into a push-up position with your hands wider than shoulder-width apart.

- Bend your body at the waist and lift your heels off the floor, keeping your back straight so your body forms an upside-down V-shape. The top of your head should be pointing toward the ground.

- Bend at your elbows to lower your head toward the floor. Then push back explosively to the start position. Repeat.

- Do this 15 times for a set and perform three sets.

EXERCISE 8: PLANK

Targets all core muscles

- Fully extend your arms and plant your hands directly under your shoulders (slightly wider than shoulder-width) like you're about to do a push-up.

- Plant your toes into the floor and squeeze your glutes to stabilize your body.

- Neutralize your neck and spine. Your head should be in line with your back.

- Keep your body straight, like a plank! This means being mindful that your butt isn't sticking up too far in the air and that your hips aren't sinking too close to the ground.

- Hold for 20 seconds, remembering to breathe and tighten your core.

- Do this three to five times.

EXERCISE 9: FLUTTER KICKS
Targets the lower abs

- Lie on your back and extend your legs up to a 45-degree angle.

- Keep your arms straight and in line with the floor, with your palms facing down. Lift your head, neck, and shoulders slightly off the ground. Do not tuck your chin.

- Keep your legs straight and your toes pointed. Now start lowering one leg.

- Raise your lowered leg and lower the other, thus "fluttering" the legs.

- Alternate the legs and continue for 30 seconds for a set. Perform four sets.

EXERCISE 10: SIDE PLANK
Targets the obliques/sides

- Lie on one side, supporting your upper body on your forearm.

- Lift your hips, keeping your weight supported on your forearm and the side of your foot with your other hand on your upper-facing hip.

- Slowly lower your hip to just above the ground but without touching the ground.

- To make this more challenging, lift the upper-facing leg into the air while you dip your hip to the ground.

- Switch sides and repeat. Do this 10 times on each side for a set (20 times total). Perform four sets.

Stretching

Stretching is the part that everyone tends to skip but is probably the most important part of your exercise routine. This is especially true for those who do not exercise often and whose joints and muscles aren't as flexible as those who move their bodies regularly. Skipping the stretch puts you at risk for injury as tight muscles are more likely to be pulled. Also, it's harder for your muscles to engage and contract the way they should when they are not stretched, making your workout less effective.

Here are my top three tips for stretching:

- I recommend at least stretching the quads, hamstrings, hip flexors, and shoulders as these tend to be most vulnerable to pulls and strains.

- Remain static and do not "bounce" into your stretch. With your muscles so extended in a stretching position, this can provoke rather than prevent a tear.

- Gaining flexibility will be uncomfortable during a stretching routine (but should never be painful!). Remember to breathe through the discomfort while holding your stretch for one minute per muscle group.

Sleep

Studies show that less sleep leads to increased hunger the next day and increased fat deposits around your waistline. Also, when you feel more fatigued and have less energy, you are less inclined to care about prepping meals and packing snacks. Everything is laborious and cumbersome when you're run down, including going to the gym or taking that run. And typically, you will eat out more and make poorer choices because you're too tired to think about healthy food. Finally, when you're sleep-deprived, your hunger hormone—ghrelin—increases, and your leptin (which suppresses your appetite) decreases. So less sleep means you are more vulnerable to hunger pangs and binges.

It is important to note that everyone is different when it comes to sleep. Some of us can get away with six hours, while others need nine. It depends on your age and level of physical exertion. This may come as a surprise to you, but I recommend people get more sleep than more exercise, as sufficient sleep impacts weight loss.

Start committing to a certain number of hours (six to eight at least—whatever feels best) per night.

Start committing to this for one to two days a week. If 10 p.m. is bedtime rather than midnight, be realistic about it. An hour before bedtime, start shutting down and removing stimulants in your environment. Studies show that the blue LED light transmitted from your TV, computer, and phone (like when you're scrolling through Instagram while lying in bed) delays the onset of the deep REM sleep you need to recover from the day and disrupts your circadian rhythm. Once electronics are off, do something to prepare yourself for quality sleep, like reading a book or taking a hot bath. Then work yourself up to following that pattern most nights of the week.

Stress

When we feel stressed or upset, our body craves the hormone dopamine, which allows us to feel pleasure and happiness. Since food (especially sweets and comfort foods) tends to give us these feelings and our brains know this, we become wired to reach for food when we feel emotional. You can avoid this impulse by following my recommended eating principles, including eating enough fiber, adding protein to your meals and snacks, and eating every three to four hours to control hunger hormones.

However, as we know, things happen, and many times you are one bad meeting, 12-hour workday, or stressful deadline away from an evening buffet in your refrigerator. The longer you ignore these eating cues, the weaker the signals get. But how can you make this happen? I have a mantra to help when emotional eating starts to creep in outside the usual eating times: distance, delay, and distract.

Distance yourself from the food you're thinking of having, which delays the onset of excess eating. Then delay. Take 10 deep breaths and ask yourself if you really need to eat that food. If you decide you do need it, go ahead and eat. If not, then distract. Distract yourself with another activity you enjoy, such as listening to music, reading a book, searching for your next vacation, taking a relaxing bubble bath, or going for a walk. Otherwise, that thought will linger in your head, which is destructive to your mental health and morale. The easiest thing for many people is to remove trigger foods from their home entirely. However, simply managing your stress could be enough.

Healthy Habits

New habits can be difficult and even discouraging to stick to long-term, so it's daunting to take them on when on the journey to controlling weight and health. However, adopting habits is the key to consistency, which is vital to reversing insulin resistance. Here are some healthy habits to consider during your weight loss efforts.

1. **Start slowly.** You wouldn't go from zero weightlifting experience to deadlifting 300 pounds just because that's your goal. Same with lifestyle habits. Science and my experience show it takes three months to form a habit, so don't expect to overhaul your diet and lifestyle overnight. You may not be able to adhere to a full exercise program consistently right away, so start with two days a week of exercise and work your way up. If you rarely eat fruits and vegetables as snacks, for example, add a single serving one or two times a week until you are eating them every day.

2. **Stay hydrated.** A study done by *Physiology and Behavior* found that people misinterpreted their thirst for hunger 62 percent of the time. That's pretty often! Over time, this can lead us to open the refrigerator for snacks (especially high-sugar snacks) when we should reach for water. This can create sneaky weight gain and unfavorable blood glucose readings. The best course of action, in this case, is to drink enough throughout the day and stay hydrated.

3. **Allow yourself to indulge.** I've always maintained that healthy eating isn't just about an eating plan full of nutritious foods but also about having a healthy relationship with food. This means not fearing the foods you love. Your favorite desserts, fast food, and childhood dishes can and should fit into your diet plan without you fearing them or forbidding yourself from having them. I speak more about this and the "80/20 principle" later in the chapter.

4. **Start your day with breakfast within 90 minutes of waking.** I've found my successful clients eat a good breakfast. Breakfast drives your entire day by jump-starting your metabolism, keeping you full until lunchtime, and preventing you from overeating later in the day.

5. **Always plan and be prepared.** One of the top reasons people fall away from their routine and back into the old habits that leave them stuck is they did not set themselves up for success. They have a meal plan but did not prep their meals ahead of time and went for fast food on their lunch break instead. Their exercise routine is built and ready to go, but they did not make time in their schedule to go to the gym. Next thing you know, it's been a week without any exercise. Be sure to make time for new habits, a diet plan, and realistic exercise that fits into your day.

HABIT TRACKER

Some people find it helpful to better adhere to new habits when they can record their progress, so I have provided this habit tracker to do just that. The example provided concerns hydration, but you can use it for just about anything you want to stick to, such as amount of time spent exercising, hours of sleep you get in a night, and other similar healthy habits. Just make sure to establish a daily goal to shoot for along with your habit (such as 80 ounces of water) and be honest in what you were able to achieve.

Habit	M	Tu	W	Th	F	Sat	S
Drink more water (80 ounces a day)	80	70	80	60	70	80	40

Tips for Success

Preparing all or most of your own meals may sound terrifying, especially if you've become comfortable with ordering in or eating out. In this section, I go over strategies to set yourself up for success as you tackle these meal plans, shortcuts you can take to save time, and staying on track during those times you need to deviate from the recipes in this book.

Meal Planning and Prepping

Having a plan is pretty much a nonnegotiable step to weight loss success. Luckily, I've done all the work for you with meal plans to guide you in your preparation. Shopping lists are also included, but you must make time to shop for your meals. I recommend doing this on a Sunday or other day that is free of work and other obligations.

Now, the part that sours most people: making time to cook. They think they must be Wolfgang Puck, slaving the week away in their kitchen, to meal prep properly. Not the case! The recipes in this book are simple, and I provide guidance on how to prep your meals so the cooking process is easier and faster. It's also a game-changer to batch cook your meals all at once. This cuts down on your cooking frequency and keeps you prepared with healthy meals ready to go.

Cooking Shortcuts

Even though I provide delicious recipes in this book, you can always use shortcuts when you don't have your usual energy to cook. Cooking in bulk on the days you feel energetic provides a safety net for the days you don't. You can even freeze some meals to prevent food waste if you want prepared meals in your back pocket for a rainy day. The use of canned and frozen fruits and vegetables also dramatically reduces prep and cook times without compromising nutritional value. Finally, one of my favorite hacks is buying a rotisserie chicken for recipes with cooked chicken. All you have to do is remove the amount of chicken you need for the recipe without taking the time to prepare it yourself.

STAYING ON TRACK WHEN EATING OUT

Don't worry; I get it. You have a life. I do not expect you to follow the recipes and meals in this book every day for the rest of your life. Celebrations, outings with friends and family, and holidays will come up, and I am a huge advocate for enjoying these indulgences in food without guilt. This is how you maintain a healthy relationship with food. However, how do you stay on track when eating out? Here are some tips:

1. **Don't go to a restaurant starving.** Although it may be tempting to get your money's worth and go to your favorite Italian spot with an empty stomach to ensure you finish your pasta entree, this can quickly boost your calories. I recommend drinking a protein shake or eating a light snack like fermented vegetables before going out to eat to prevent overeating foods that may not be the best for your goals.

2. **Know your menu terms.** Even if it doesn't outright say something is "fried" on the menu, terms like "crispy," "battered," or "crunchy" almost always mean something in that dish was submerged in hot oil. If the cooking method or an ingredient of something you want to order is unfamiliar, make sure to ask.

3. **Watch the condiments.** Cream-based sauces like alfredo, ranch, mayonnaise, and sour cream tend to be high in calories and saturated fat. Instead, go for tomato- and oil-based sauces and dressings like marinara, pesto, tzatziki (yogurt-based), and vinaigrettes for a dose of healthy fats to go with your meal.

4. **Be aware of your portions.** Only order what you can eat! This is another reason it's good not to go to a restaurant hungry. You can ask the server for a to-go container ahead of time and put half of your meal in the box and out of sight until you get home. You may find that not only did you not need to eat that oversized portion, but you also made the smart, economical move to have lunch for tomorrow!

5. **Don't be afraid to sub your side.** If there is an option to substitute a side like French fries or onion rings with a salad or fruit, try to balance your meal with that option, especially if the main dish is already high in calories, fat, and sodium.

Lifelong Health

It is important to know that even when you reach your goal of reversing insulin resistance, losing weight, and improving your health, it doesn't mean that you can abandon all these habits you worked so hard to adopt. Although you may have the luxury of increasing your calories harmlessly by 300 to 500 daily, pretty much everything else you've done to achieve your progress will remain the same. If you want to continue to keep insulin resistance and diabetes at bay, it's important to keep visceral fat and excess fat off your body, keep waist circumference below the ranges mentioned, and maintain a nutritious, anti-inflammatory diet. Exercise is a great tool for helping you maintain your weight and keep your heart healthy. You may be wondering when you get to enjoy your indulgent, favorite meals again.

It is counterintuitive to compromise your quality of life for the sake of health. Healthy eating is about not just choosing the right foods but also having a good relationship with food. That means enjoying all the foods you love without guilt or shame. The minute you put a "no" on a food, when the time comes to give yourself the green light, you will almost always overeat that food. Please know that all foods have a place in your eating plan, but some are higher in sugar and calories and should be consumed infrequently. Therefore, I preach what I call the 80/20 principle. This simply means you follow the plan 80 percent of the week and the remaining 20 percent you can use for social interactions or personal indulgences.

The bottom line is when you begin to adopt the habits in this book, remember to go in with the mindset that these will be ongoing habits. These habits are long-haul changes—you cannot just abandon them the second you see results if you wish to maintain them.

CHAPTER 3

Breakfast

Mango-Avocado-Spinach Smoothie

Makes 1 serving
Prep time: 5 minutes

Recent research has shown that consuming avocado has been associated with lower body weight and waist circumference, which is critical to controlling insulin resistance. Avocados, spinach, and mango are also good sources of fiber and help control hunger and manage weight.

3 cups baby spinach
  leaves
1 cup 1 percent milk
⅓ avocado
½ cup frozen mango
½ cup low-fat cottage
  cheese

Combine the spinach, milk, avocado, mango, and cottage cheese in a blender and blend until smooth.

Leftover Tip: Refrigerate plastic-wrapped leftover avocado after brushing the cut side with a squeeze of lime or lemon juice to prevent oxidation.

Per serving (24 fluid ounces): Calories 450; Fat: 22g; Carbohydrates: 40g; Fiber: 8g; Sugar: 25g; Protein: 27g; Sodium: 307mg

Mixed Berry Yogurt Smoothie

Makes 1 serving
Prep time: 5 minutes

Greek yogurt is a great source of probiotics, the good bacteria that keep our gut healthy. Some evidence suggests those with healthier guts have better blood glucose control. I've added protein powder to provide 20 grams of protein.

1 cup 1 percent milk

1 cup frozen mixed berries

½ cup plain 2 percent Greek yogurt

1 teaspoon ground cinnamon

1 scoop vanilla protein powder (whey, soy, pea, or rice)

Combine the milk, berries, yogurt, cinnamon, and protein powder in a blender and blend until smooth.

Substitution Tip: If you don't eat dairy, you can use non-dairy yogurt instead. Just read the label to be sure it is the type that includes probiotics.

Per serving (24 fluid ounces): Calories 358; Fat: 4g; Carbohydrates: 46g; Fiber: 6g; Sugar: 30g; Protein: 27g; Sodium: 257mg

Orange-Carrot Smoothie

Makes 1 serving
Prep time: 5 minutes

Several small studies have associated cinnamon consumption with better blood sugar control. This warm spice contains a compound called cinnamaldehyde, which may help reduce inflammation. Here it's combined with nutrient rich oranges and carrots for a strong morning start.

1 cup low-fat oat beverage

1 orange, peeled and segmented

1 carrot

1 scoop vanilla protein powder (whey, soy, pea, or rice, with at least 20 grams of protein per serving)

1 teaspoon chia seeds

½ teaspoon ground cinnamon

⅛ teaspoon crushed ginger

Combine the oat beverage, orange, carrot, protein powder, chia seeds, cinnamon, and ginger in a blender and blend until smooth.

Meal Prep Tip: As with any smoothie in this book, you can double the recipe if you want to save some for the future. Refrigerate one portion in an airtight container and eat within 24 hours.

Per serving (24 fluid ounces): Calories 268; Fat: 5g; Carbohydrates: 40g; Fiber: 7g; Sugar: 15g; Protein: 20g; Sodium: 251mg

Oat-Apple Spiced Smoothie

Makes 1 serving
Prep time: 5 minutes

Oats are one of the most common, economical sources of soluble fiber. When mixed with the water content of your digestive system, this fiber forms a gel-like substance in the gut that keeps you feeling fuller for longer. This type of satiety can help prevent overeating throughout the day. This spiced smoothie is a fun and deliciously different way to enjoy your morning oats.

1 cup low-fat oat beverage

¼ cup cooked quick oats

¼ cup unsweetened applesauce

1 scoop vanilla protein powder (whey, soy, pea, or rice, with at least 20 grams of protein per serving)

¼ teaspoon ground cinnamon

Combine the oat beverage, oats, applesauce, protein powder, and cinnamon in a blender and blend until smooth.

Ingredient Tip: When you look for your oat beverages, look for 100 calories per serving because the calorie content of oat beverages can vary wildly between brands.

Per serving (16 fluid ounces): Calories: 217; Fat: 4g; Carbohydrates: 28g; Fiber: 3g; Sugar: 6g; Protein: 19g; Sodium: 210mg

Superfoods Smoothie Bowl

Makes 1 serving
Prep time: 5 minutes

This smoothie bowl is easy to make at home and contains numerous superfoods to boost your health. I like to top it with cacao nibs, which are available in most grocery stores. Cacao is a delicious source of antioxidants that I regularly add to recipes. I also love to enjoy some cacao nibs as a snack when a sweet tooth strikes. Cacao contains heart-healthy antioxidant compounds.

FOR THE BASE
1 cup frozen
   strawberries
½ cup plain 2 percent
   Greek yogurt
1 scoop of vanilla
   protein powder (whey,
   soy, pea, or rice with
   at least 20 grams of
   protein per serving)
2 tablespoons
   1 percent milk
½ tablespoon ground
   cinnamon
½ tablespoon pure
   vanilla extract
Pinch sea salt

FOR THE BOWL
½ cup blueberries
1 teaspoon cacao nibs
1 teaspoon chia seeds
1 teaspoon shredded
   coconut

1. **To make the base:** Combine the strawberries, yogurt, protein powder, milk, cinnamon, vanilla, and salt in a blender and blend until you reach a thick consistency.

2. **To make the bowl:** Pour the mixture into a serving bowl, add the blueberries, cacao nibs, chia seeds, and coconut, and serve.

Meal Prep Tip: Want to make this a grab-and-go breakfast for days you want to sleep in? Create this recipe in to-go containers or mason jars to make it instantly portable.

Per serving (16 fluid ounces plus toppings): Calories 353; Fat: 3g; Carbohydrates: 51g; Fiber: 10g; Sugar: 24g; Protein: 32g; Sodium: 323mg

Queso Fresco, Tomato, and Avocado Wrap

Makes 1 serving
Prep time: 10 minutes

Queso fresco is a common cheese in Latin cuisine renowned for its creamy texture and tangy flavor. Don't be fooled by the simplicity of this recipe; the combination of the cheese with the avocado and spice of arugula makes this meal a delight.

1 tablespoon olive oil mayonnaise dressing
1 (10-by-8-inch) whole-grain lavash bread
¼ avocado
4 tomato slices
6 basil leaves
1 cup arugula
2 ounces queso fresco, sliced

1. Spread the mayonnaise over the lavash bread to about 1 inch from the edges. Mash the avocado on top of the mayonnaise, spreading it out in the same dimensions.

2. Layer the tomatoes, basil, arugula, and cheese on the avocado. Roll the bread into a wrap, starting at the short end, and halve it widthwise.

3. Enjoy.

Cooking Tip: When using queso fresco, taste the dish before adding additional salt. The salt content of the cheese is often significant enough to add flavor.

Per serving (1 wrap): Calories: 522; Fat: 29g; Carbohydrates: 46g; Fiber: 11g; Sugar: 10g; Protein: 21g; Sodium: 624mg

Primavera Frittata

Makes 4 servings
Prep time: 10 minutes / **Cook time:** 20 minutes

We use both whole eggs and egg whites to balance the macronutrients in this recipe. Despite what you may have heard, most of the nutrients are in the yolk of the egg, including choline, an essential nutrient for brain health.

1 tablespoon extra-virgin olive oil

1 small yellow onion, diced

1 cup cherry tomatoes, halved

1 small red bell pepper, seeded and diced

4 scallions, both white and green parts, diced

¼ cup chopped fresh basil

6 large eggs

1½ cups egg whites

½ tablespoon sea salt

¼ teaspoon freshly ground black pepper

1. In a large nonstick skillet, heat the oil for 1 minute over medium heat.

2. Add the onion, cherry tomatoes, and bell pepper and cook for 4 minutes.

3. Add the scallions and basil and cook for 2 minutes.

4. While the vegetables cook, whisk the eggs, egg whites, salt, and pepper in a medium bowl.

5. Pour the egg mixture into the skillet and mix all the ingredients well. Cover and cook for about 10 minutes over medium heat, or until the frittata becomes puffy and firm.

6. Slice the frittata into 4 servings and enjoy warm.

7. Refrigerate leftovers in an airtight container for up to 4 days.

Ingredient Tip: If you don't want to waste egg yolks from whole eggs to get to the egg whites, buy a carton of egg whites in the egg and dairy section of your grocery store.

Per serving (¼ sliced): Calories: 209; Fat: 11g; Carbohydrates: 7g; Fiber: 2g; Sugar: 4g; Protein: 20g; Sodium: 264mg

Canadian Bacon, Spinach, and Cheese Quiches

Makes 6 servings
Prep time: 10 minutes / **Cook time:** 40 minutes

Think beyond breakfast for this delicious recipe! The egg, ham, and cheese contribute a healthy dose of protein to keep you satiated until your next meal. This mouthwatering quiche is also a satisfying afternoon snack.

Nonstick cooking spray
1 tablespoon extra-virgin olive oil
3 cups frozen spinach, thawed, liquid squeezed out, and chopped
½ cup diced yellow onion
6 ounces sliced mushrooms
6 large eggs
1½ cups egg whites
3 ounces precooked Canadian bacon, diced
3 ounces shredded part-skim mozzarella cheese
1 teaspoon sea salt
¼ teaspoon freshly ground black pepper

1. Preheat the oven to 350°F. Spray a 12-cup muffin tin with nonstick cooking spray and set it aside.

2. In a large nonstick skillet, heat the oil for 1 minute over medium heat.

3. Add the spinach, onion, and mushrooms, and cook for 10 minutes, or until most of the water from the vegetables is evaporated. Set the mixture aside and let it cool for 3 minutes.

4. In a medium bowl, combine the eggs, egg whites, Canadian bacon, cheese, salt, pepper, and the vegetables.

5. Evenly divide the mixture between the 12 muffin cups, leaving a ½-inch space at the top of each quiche. Bake for 20 to 25 minutes, or until puffed and lightly browned.

6. Enjoy immediately or allow the quiches to cool and refrigerate leftovers in an airtight container for up to 5 days.

Cooking Tip: Use foil or paper muffin liners in your muffin tin for easy cleanup.

Per serving (2 quiches): Calories: 209; Fat: 10g; Carbohydrates: 7g; Fiber: 3g; Sugar: 3g; Protein: 23g; Sodium: 425mg

Savory Rolled Oat Bowl with Fried Egg

Makes 4 servings
Prep time: 10 minutes / **Cook time:** 30 minutes

Do you need your oats to be sweet to get your dose of soluble fiber? Not at all! This savory oat recipe is a nutritious, filling meal with a hefty portion of veggies. I am always thinking of creative ways to add more vegetables to my diet, especially at breakfast, and these oats are a great way to do it.

4 cups water
1 cup steel-cut oats
¾ teaspoon sea salt, divided
½ cup shredded parmesan cheese
1 tablespoon extra-virgin olive oil
10 ounces quartered zucchini
10 ounces sliced cremini mushrooms
½ teaspoon MSG (Accent)
¼ teaspoon freshly ground black pepper
4 scallions, both white and green parts, sliced
4 large eggs fried in nonstick cooking spray

1. Bring the water to a boil in a medium saucepan over high heat. Add the oats and ¼ teaspoon of salt, reduce the heat to low, cover, and simmer for 20 minutes until the liquid is absorbed.

2. Remove the saucepan from the heat, stir in the cheese, and set the pan aside.

3. Heat the oil in a medium skillet over medium heat. Add the zucchini, mushrooms, remaining ½ teaspoon of salt, MSG, and pepper and sauté until soft, about 6 minutes.

4. Fill 4 bowls with ¾ cup of oats and ¾ cup of veggies. Sprinkle each with scallion and top with 1 fried egg. Serve.

5. Refrigerate leftovers in an airtight container for up to 4 days.

Variation Tip: If you want to add extra, non-starchy veggies to this meal, go for it! Non-starchy vegetables have a negligible effect on blood glucose levels.

Per serving (¾ cup oats + ¾ veggies on top + egg):
Calories 363; Fat: 15g; Carbohydrates: 40g; Fiber: 7g; Sugar: 5g; Protein: 18g; Sodium: 613mg

Pumpkin–Greek Yogurt Overnight Oats

Makes 4 servings
Prep time: 10 minutes

This fun fall twist on overnight oats can be enjoyed year-round. These oats require no cooking and can be thrown together in no time and used for breakfast on multiple mornings.

2 cups plain 2 percent Greek yogurt

2 cups 1 percent milk (or milk of choice)

1 cup rolled oats

1 cup canned pumpkin puree

¼ cup psyllium husk

1 scoop vanilla protein powder (whey, soy, pea, or rice, with at least 20 grams of protein per serving)

1 tablespoon pure vanilla extract

1 tablespoon ground cinnamon

½ teaspoon sea salt

1. Evenly divide the yogurt, milk, oats, pumpkin, psyllium husk, protein powder, vanilla, cinnamon, and salt between 4 (12-ounce) lidded jars.

2. Use a spoon to stir the ingredients well until fully incorporated.

3. Seal the jars and allow them to sit for 4 hours up to overnight in the refrigerator, until the oats have thickened, before enjoying.

4. Refrigerate leftovers in an airtight container for up to 4 days.

Serving Tip: This breakfast can also be used as a filling snack.

Per serving (1½ cup serving): Calories 300; Fat: 5g; Carbohydrates: 44g; Fiber: 10g; Sugar: 18g; Protein: 19g; Sodium: 315mg

Butternut Squash Pancakes

Makes 4 servings
Prep time: 10 minutes / **Cook time:** 35 minutes

Butternut squash is a starchy vegetable with only 12 grams of carbs per 100 grams. This is the lowest carbohydrate content of all the starchy veggies, so it won't spike your blood sugar. Butternut squash contributes a beautiful sweetness to these pancakes without added sugar.

FOR THE SAUCE
4 cups frozen mixed berries, thawed
1 cup water
¾ cup monk fruit sweetener
3 whole cloves
2 cinnamon sticks
Peel of one orange, washed

FOR THE PANCAKES
8 ounces butternut squash, cubed
½ cup 1 percent milk
½ cup 2 percent cottage cheese
2 large eggs
1 cup quick oats
2 tablespoons monk fruit sweetener
2 teaspoons baking soda
½ tablespoon pure vanilla extract
½ tablespoon ground cinnamon
Nonstick cooking spray

TO MAKE THE SAUCE

1. Add the thawed berries and water to a blender and blend until smooth.

2. In a small saucepan, mix the pureed berries, sweetener, cloves, cinnamon sticks, and orange peel and bring to a boil over medium heat.

3. Reduce the heat to low and simmer the sauce until it thickens and is reduced by half, about 20 minutes.

4. Remove the sauce from the heat and let it cool. Strain the sauce through a fine-mesh sieve and store it in a jar with a tight seal in the refrigerator for up to 1 week.

TO MAKE THE PANCAKES

5. Combine the squash, milk, cottage cheese, eggs, oats, sweetener, baking soda, vanilla, and cinnamon in a high-speed blender and blend on high until completely smooth, about 30 seconds.

6. Coat a griddle or a large nonstick skillet with nonstick cooking spray and heat it over medium-low heat.

7. Once the skillet is hot, working in batches, add ⅓ cup of the batter to the skillet for each pancake and cook for 3 minutes, or until the pancakes slightly puff up and you see a few bubbles along the edges. Flip and cook the pancakes for 3 minutes more.

8. Transfer the pancakes to a cooling rack or plate and repeat until you've used up all the batter. Top each pancake with 1 tablespoon of berry sauce and serve warm.

9. Refrigerate leftovers in an airtight container for up to 5 days.

Cooking Tip: The sauce for these pancakes consists of frozen berries and monk fruit sweetener, so you still get the sweetness you crave from syrup without all the added sugar.

Pancake per serving (2 pancakes and 2 tablespoons sauce): Calories 199; Fat: 5g; Carbohydrates: 29g; Fiber: 5g; Sugar: 8g; Protein: 11g; Sodium: 769mg

Blueberry High-Fiber Muffins

Makes 12 servings
Prep time: 10 minutes / **Cook time:** 30 minutes

Did you know that blueberries contain the highest antioxidant content of any berry? The main antioxidants in blueberries are called anthocyanins and may help control glucose.

¾ cup 2 percent milk

3 tablespoons chia seeds

Nonstick cooking spray

1 cup all-purpose flour

1 cup quick oats

2 scoops vanilla protein powder (whey, soy, pea, or rice)

½ cup psyllium husk

¼ cup monk fruit sweetener

1 tablespoon ground cinnamon

1 teaspoon baking soda

1 teaspoon baking powder

1 teaspoon sea salt

1 cup 2 percent plain Greek yogurt

2 large eggs

3 tablespoons canola oil

1 tablespoon pure vanilla extract

2 cups fresh blueberries

1. In a small microwave-safe bowl, warm the milk in the microwave for about 1 minute. Add the chia seeds and soak for 5 minutes.

2. Preheat the oven to 350°F. Line a 12-cup muffin tin with paper cups and spray them with nonstick cooking spray. Set it aside.

3. In a large bowl, whisk the flour, oats, protein powder, psyllium husk, sweetener, cinnamon, baking soda, baking powder, and salt until well blended. Set it aside.

4. In a medium bowl, whisk the chia seed mixture, yogurt, eggs, oil, and vanilla until well combined.

5. Add the wet ingredients to the dry ingredients and stir until just combined. Stir in the blueberries.

6. Spoon the batter evenly inside the muffin cups and bake for 20 minutes, or until a toothpick inserted in the center of a muffin comes out clean.

7. Serve warm, or store leftovers in an airtight container for up to 4 days.

Ingredient Tip: You can use protein powder from any protein source, but the amount is key. Make sure 2 scoops add up to 60 grams of protein. This recipe was tested using whey protein isolate.

Per serving (1 muffin): Calories: 192; Fat: 7g; Carbohydrates: 24g; Fiber: 5g; Sugar: 5g; Protein: 8g; Sodium: 285mg

CHAPTER 4

Mains

Gut Healthy Chopped Salad

Makes 6 servings
Prep time: 15 minutes

This salad contains both probiotics and prebiotics, making it a powerhouse for gut health. Probiotics are the good bacteria that work to keep our gut healthy, and prebiotics are the "food" these bacteria eat to help them thrive and multiply.

3 carrots, thinly sliced

5 radishes, thinly sliced

2 cups frozen corn, thawed

1 (15½-ounce) can low-sodium black beans, drained and rinsed

1½ cups sauerkraut with live cultures

1 avocado, peeled, pitted, and cubed

1 cup jicama, cut into small strips

½ cup chopped cilantro

¼ cup diced red onion

3 tablespoons rice vinegar

2 tablespoons extra-virgin olive oil

1½ teaspoons sea salt

½ teaspoon freshly ground black pepper

1. Combine the carrots, radishes, corn, black beans, sauerkraut, avocado, jicama, cilantro, onion, vinegar, oil, salt, and pepper in a large bowl. Mix until well combined and enjoy.

2. Refrigerate this salad in an airtight container for up to 4 days.

Serving Tip: Pair this salad with your favorite protein for satiety; I love it with the Blackened Salmon (see page 74).

Per serving (1½ cups): Calories 244; Fat: 10g; Carbohydrates: 32g; Fiber: 10g; Sugar: 5g; Protein: 7g; Sodium: 555mg

Latino Mediterranean Salad

Makes 4 servings
Prep time: 10 minutes

I've created a take on the classic Greek salad with a Latin touch. This recipe uses queso fresco instead of feta and avocado to add an even bigger heart-healthy punch in addition to the olive oil.

10 ounces queso fresco, cubed

2 cups cubed Persian cucumber

1 cup cherry tomatoes

1 medium avocado, peeled, pitted, and cubed

½ cup kalamata olives, pitted

¼ cup sliced red onion (optional)

¼ cup chopped fresh basil

2 tablespoons freshly squeezed lemon juice

½ tablespoon extra-virgin olive oil

1 teaspoon dried oregano

1. Combine the queso fresco, cucumber, tomatoes, avocado, olives, onion (if using), basil, lemon juice, olive oil, and oregano in a large bowl. Mix until well combined and enjoy.

2. Refrigerate leftovers in an airtight container for up to 4 days.

Cooking Tip: Queso fresco provides high-quality protein, so it can act as your protein choice.

Per serving (1½ cups): Calories 318; Fat: 26g; Carbohydrates: 12g; Fiber: 5g; Sugar: 5g; Protein: 12g; Sodium: 680mg

Warm Turkey Cheese Wrap

Makes 1 serving
Prep time: 5 minutes / **Cook time:** 10 minutes

Who doesn't love a nice, crispy sandwich for lunch? This wrap is a take on a panini, but there is no need for a panini press to make this sandwich a hit.

1 tablespoon olive oil
  mayonnaise dressing
1 (10-by-8-inch)
  whole-grain lavash
  bread
1 cup arugula
3 ounces turkey slices
1½ ounces sliced Swiss
  cheese

1. Spread the mayonnaise over the lavash bread to about 1 inch from the edges.

2. Place the arugula over ⅓ of the bread and top with the turkey and cheese. Fold one end of the bread over the other end, like you are making a sandwich.

3. Place a large skillet over medium-high heat, place the sandwich in the skillet, put a small lid on top to weigh it down, and cook for 2 to 3 minutes. Flip to the other side and cook for another 2 to 3 minutes.

4. Enjoy.

Serving Tip: If you choose to make this melt ahead of time, wrap it in foil and pop it in the oven or toaster oven for quick reheating.

Per serving (1 serving): Calories 444; Fat: 22g; Carbohydrates: 27g; Fiber: 4g; Sugar: 7g; Protein: 33g; Sodium: 911mg

Turkey and Vegetable Meatloaf

Makes 4 servings
Prep time: 20 minutes / **Cook time:** 55 minutes

Meatloaf is an American culinary icon. However, it's not always associated with health. That all changes with this meatloaf because it uses ground turkey, a lean source of protein that is low in saturated fat. Each slice also gives you a serving of vegetables.

Nonstick cooking spray
2 celery stalks
2 carrots
1 medium yellow onion
10 ounces cremini or white mushrooms
1 large red bell pepper, seeded
1 pound 93 percent lean ground turkey
2 large eggs
½ cup quick oats
½ cup shredded parmesan cheese
1 tablespoon dried oregano
1½ teaspoon sea salt
1 teaspoon freshly ground black pepper
1 teaspoon MSG (optional)

1. Preheat the oven to 375°F. Spray a 9-by-5-inch loaf pan with nonstick cooking spray.

2. Using a food processor, pulse the celery, carrots, onion, mushrooms, and bell pepper until finely chopped.

3. In a large bowl, combine the turkey, chopped vegetables, eggs, oats, cheese, oregano, salt, pepper, and MSG (if using). Use your hands to mix everything, ensuring that the ingredients are well distributed.

4. Press the meat mixture into the prepared loaf pan, cover with aluminum foil, and place in the oven on the middle rack. Bake the meatloaf for 40 minutes.

5. Remove the aluminum foil and bake uncovered for another 15 minutes, or until golden brown.

6. Remove the meatloaf from the oven and then from the loaf pan and let it cool for 10 minutes.

7. Slice and serve warm.

Ingredient Tip: The use of MSG reduces sodium intake by 40 percent. Contrary to popular belief, MSG is perfectly safe to eat when added to your diet.

Per serving (360 grams): Calories 352; Fat: 17g; Carbohydrates: 20g; Fiber: 5g; Sugar: 6g; Protein: 33g; Sodium: 819mg

Roasted Eggplant, Butternut Squash, and Sirloin Steak Stew

Makes 6 servings
Prep time: 10 minutes / **Cook time:** 30 minutes

Stews are comfort food that usually take hours to develop deep, warming flavor. This one cooks in 30 minutes. The canned and frozen produce still provide good nutrition but drastically cut down on the usual prep time.

3 cups eggplant, cut into 1-inch cubes

3 cups butternut squash, cut into 1-inch cubes

Nonstick cooking spray

1 tablespoon extra-virgin olive oil, divided

1 medium red onion, diced

1 tablespoon minced garlic

2 celery stalks, diced

2 carrots, sliced

1 (14½-ounce) can low-sodium diced tomatoes

½ cup low-sodium beef or chicken broth

1½ teaspoons sea salt

1 teaspoon ground cumin

½ teaspoon freshly ground black pepper

⅛ teaspoon ground cloves

2 pounds top sirloin strip steak

1 cup frozen peas

1. Preheat the oven to 400°F.

2. Spread the eggplant and butternut squash in a single layer on a baking sheet. Spray the veggies with nonstick cooking spray and roast for 25 minutes, or until golden brown. Set aside.

3. In the meantime, heat the oil in a large skillet and sauté the onion and garlic for about 2 minutes.

4. Add the celery, carrots, tomatoes, broth, salt, cumin, pepper, and cloves, and cook for 10 minutes.

5. Add the meat and cook for 10 minutes, or until no longer pink. Cut the steak into strips.

6. Add the peas and roasted eggplant and butternut squash mixture, toss gently without mashing the butternut squash, and cook for about 3 minutes until everything is heated through.

7. Refrigerate leftovers in an airtight container for up to 5 days.

Meal Prep Tip: This can be batch cooked and frozen in zip-top bags and/or airtight containers to be reheated whenever you need a quick dinner in a pinch.

Per serving (1½ cup): Calories: 390; Fat: 20g; Carbohydrates: 19g; Fiber: 6g; Sugar: 7g; Protein: 34g; Sodium: 409mg

Soy-Ginger Pork Tenderloin

Makes 4 servings
Prep time: 10 minutes, plus 30 minutes to marinate / **Cook time:** 15 minutes

It may surprise you to hear this, but pork tenderloin is a lower-calorie cut of meat than chicken breast. Here it's prepared with soy and ginger flavors. On top of that, pineapple contains an enzyme called bromelain that, when used to marinate meat, is effective at making it nice and tender.

FOR THE MARINADE
½ cup crushed pineapple
½ tablespoon sesame oil
½ cup low-sodium soy sauce
1 tablespoon minced garlic
1 tablespoon crushed ginger

1½ pounds pork tenderloin, cubed

FOR THE STIR-FRY
½ tablespoon sesame oil
1 red onion, sliced
1 pound frozen cut green beans, thawed

1 large red bell pepper, seeded and cut into strips
½ cup canned juice-packed diced pineapple
2 teaspoons cornstarch
2 tablespoons sesame seeds

TO MAKE THE MARINADE

1. In a small bowl, combine the pineapple, oil, soy sauce, garlic, and ginger.

2. Place the pork cubes in a zip-top plastic bag and pour in the marinade. Combine well, making sure all the pork is covered with the mixture, and marinate for 30 minutes.

TO MAKE THE STIR-FRY

3. In the meantime, heat the oil in a large skillet over medium heat and sauté the onion for 3 minutes. Add the green beans and bell pepper and sauté for 4 minutes, or until softened. Add the pineapple and transfer the mixture to a medium bowl with a slotted spoon.

4. Using the same skillet, cook the pork without the marinade over medium heat for 4 minutes, or until it is no longer pink.

5. Add the vegetable mixture and leftover marinade to the skillet and mix well.

6. Add the cornstarch and cook over low-medium heat for 2 to 3 minutes until the sauce thickens.

7. Serve topped with the sesame seeds.

8. Refrigerate leftovers in an airtight container for up to 5 days.

Serving Tip: If you enjoy stir-fry with rice, I recommend using black rice because of its higher fiber content and compound anthocyanins, both of which are great for blood glucose control.

Per serving (2 cups): Calories 346; Fat: 11g; Carbohydrates: 22g; Fiber: 5g; Sugar: 13g; Protein: 39g; Sodium: 356mg

Spicy Beef Burgers

Makes 4 servings
Prep time: 10 minutes / **Cook time:** 10 minutes

Who says burgers can't be nutritious? These patties are made with a Latin flavor flair, so they will taste different from any other burger you have tried. The addition of veggies to the recipe gives these burgers a nice boost of nutrients. These burgers go well with salads, on lettuce leaves, or with a side like roasted vegetables or farro.

1 pound 93 percent lean ground beef
⅓ cup finely chopped red onion
½ cup finely chopped cilantro
1 jalapeño pepper, seeded and finely chopped
1 tablespoon freshly squeezed lime juice
1 teaspoon sea salt
½ teaspoon freshly ground black pepper
Nonstick cooking spray

1. In a large bowl, combine the ground beef, onion, cilantro, jalapeño, lime juice, salt, and pepper, using your hands to mix all the ingredients well.

2. Using a ¾-cup measuring cup, form four (5½-ounce) patties and set them on a baking sheet or plate.

3. Spray a large skillet with nonstick cooking spray and place it over medium heat. Place the patties in the skillet, cover, and cook for 5 minutes on one side. Flip the patties and cook uncovered for another 5 minutes.

4. Serve warm.

5. Refrigerate leftovers in an airtight container for up to 5 days.

Ingredient Tip: Controlling the calories and fat is all about the cut of meat you use. For this recipe, I used beef that is 93 percent lean. I recommend using ground beef that is no less than 90 percent lean for any recipe.

Per serving (1 patty): Calories 156; Fat: 6g; Carbohydrates: 2g; Fiber: 0g; Sugar: 1g; Protein: 24g; Sodium: 367mg

Asparagus-Cauliflower Risotto

Makes 4 servings
Prep time: 10 minutes / **Cook time:** 15 minutes

The white rice typically used in a traditional risotto can spike blood glucose quickly, so I wanted to bring you a risotto flavor using cauliflower to replace the rice. The cheese gives the nice creaminess you look for in a classic risotto.

1 tablespoon
extra-virgin olive oil

1 medium yellow onion,
diced

10 ounces white
mushrooms, sliced

10 ounces asparagus,
chopped

1 pound cauliflower
florets, finely chopped

1 cup 1 percent milk

1 cup shredded
parmesan cheese

1 cup shredded
part-skim mozzarella

2 teaspoons sea salt

¼ teaspoon freshly
ground black pepper

1. Heat the oil in a large skillet over high heat and sauté the onion and mushrooms for 5 minutes until browned.

2. Add the asparagus and cauliflower to the skillet and cook for 4 to 5 minutes, or until the vegetables are soft.

3. Add the milk, parmesan, mozzarella, salt, and pepper and mix well. Reduce the heat to medium-low and cook for 3 minutes, or until the sauce thickens as the cheese melts.

4. Refrigerate leftovers in an airtight container for up to 3 days.

Serving Tip: Pair with a protein choice to balance the macronutrients. My favorite pairing for this risotto is sirloin steak or Blackened Salmon (see page 74). Not in the mood to chop a head of cauliflower? Use a food processor to pulse the florets or buy riced cauliflower at the grocery store.

Per serving (2 cups): Calories 302; Fat: 16g; Carbohydrates: 21g; Fiber: 5g; Sugar: 10g; Protein: 22g; Sodium: 1,275mg

Peruvian-Inspired Quinoa Pesto Bowl

Makes 4 servings
Prep time: 10 minutes / **Cook time:** 15 minutes

Of course, being Peruvian, I had to include at least one Peruvian recipe, and this is one of my favorites. Quinoa is a high-fiber, high-protein seed that is gluten-free and diabetes- and weight loss-friendly. You'll love the pesto that provides the punch of flavor and might want to use it in other recipes.

FOR THE QUINOA
2 cups low-sodium vegetable or chicken broth
2 cups frozen mixed vegetables (peas, corn, carrots, green beans), thawed
1 cup quinoa, rinsed
½ teaspoon sea salt

4 fried or poached eggs, for topping

FOR THE PESTO
1 tablespoon extra-virgin olive oil
½ cup diced red onion
1 teaspoon minced garlic
5 cups baby spinach leaves, packed

2 cup fresh basil leaves, packed
¾ cup 1 percent milk
10 ounces queso fresco (about 2 cups)
¼ cup chopped walnuts
½ teaspoon sea salt
½ teaspoon freshly ground black pepper

TO MAKE THE QUINOA

1. In a small saucepan, combine the broth, vegetables, quinoa, and salt and bring to a boil over medium-high heat. Reduce the heat to low, partially cover, and simmer for 15 minutes, or until the quinoa is cooked. Set it aside to cool.

TO MAKE THE PESTO

2. While the quinoa is cooking, heat the oil in a large skillet over medium heat. Sauté the onion until translucent, about 3 minutes. Add the garlic and sauté for 1 minute, until fragrant.

3. Stir in the spinach and basil and sauté until wilted, about 5 minutes.

4. Transfer the spinach mixture to a blender or food processor. Add the milk, queso fresco, walnuts, salt, and pepper and blend until smooth and creamy.

5. Evenly divide the quinoa between 4 serving bowls, top each with ¼ of the sauce and a fried egg, and serve.

6. If you have sauce left over, refrigerate it in an airtight container for up to 5 days.

Serving Tip: Serve the sauce poured over high-protein pasta or lean meat like salmon or chicken breast.

Per serving (¾ cup quinoa + ¼ cup pesto): Calories: 363; Fat: 16g; Carbohydrates: 39g; Fiber: 6g; Sugar: 3g; Protein: 18g; Sodium: 416mg

Pico de Gallo, Black Bean, and Chicken Bowl

Makes 4 servings
Prep time: 10 minutes

This bowl is a nutritious take on a Mexican-style dish that uses a tasty mixture of salsa and black beans. Black beans are a good source of soluble fiber for glucose regulation and hunger control.

1 pound Greek-Inspired Roasted Chicken Breast (page 104), chopped

2 (15½-ounce) cans low-sodium black beans, drained and rinsed

2 large tomatoes, diced

1 small cucumber, diced

1 jalapeño pepper, seeded and sliced

1 cup coarsely chopped cilantro

⅓ cup diced red onion

1 tablespoon freshly squeezed lime juice

1 tablespoon olive oil

1½ teaspoons sea salt

¼ teaspoon freshly ground black pepper

1. In a large bowl, combine the chicken, beans, tomatoes, cucumber, jalapeño, cilantro, onion, lime juice, olive oil, salt, and pepper, and mix well.

2. Refrigerate leftovers in an airtight container for up to 5 days.

Cooking Tip: If you cannot buy low-sodium canned beans, rinse your beans in water to reduce the amount of sodium. I cook with and recommend canned beans often as they are a convenient way to use a low-cost, nutrient-packed food.

Per serving (1¾ cup pico de gallo + 4 ounces chicken): Calories 417; Fat: 8g; Carbohydrates: 37g; Fiber: 13g; Sugar: 4g; Protein: 48g; Sodium: 529mg

Fried Farro with Shrimp and Veggies

Makes 4 servings
Prep time: 10 minutes / **Cook time:** 20 minutes

Who doesn't love fried rice? Farro is an ancient whole grain high in protein and fiber compared to traditional white rice. I doubled the usual amount of vegetables in classic fried rice to lower the carbohydrate content and boost the fiber.

3 large eggs

⅛ teaspoon sea salt

Nonstick cooking spray

1 tablespoon sesame oil

3 celery stalks, diced

½ cup diced red onion

½ teaspoon minced garlic

1 teaspoon crushed ginger

1 pound large (21/25 count) shrimp, peeled and deveined

3 cups frozen mixed vegetables (peas, corn, carrots, green beans), thawed

3 tablespoons low-sodium soy sauce

½ teaspoon sea salt

3 cups Flavorful Farro (see page 108)

4 scallions, both green and white parts, diced

1. In a small bowl, whisk the eggs and salt until combined.

2. Heat a medium skillet over medium heat and spray it lightly with nonstick cooking spray. Pour the eggs into the skillet and cook for about 5 minutes until set and cooked. Set the skillet aside to cool for 5 minutes and chop the omelet into 1-inch pieces.

3. Heat the sesame oil in a large skillet over medium heat.

4. Sauté the celery, red onion, garlic, and ginger for 3 minutes, or until softened.

5. Increase the heat to high, add the shrimp and veggies, and cook for 3 minutes. Add the soy sauce and salt, and toss to combine.

6. Add the farro, scallions, and egg and mix well. Cook for another 2 minutes and serve.

Meal Prep Tip: This is a great dish to meal prep on a Sunday and eat throughout the week as it can be stored in the refrigerator for up to 5 days.

Per serving (2¼ cups): Calories 435; Fat: 11g; Carbohydrates: 50g; Fiber: 14g; Sugar: 6g; Protein: 30g; Sodium: 1,383mg

Blackened Salmon

Makes 4 servings
Prep time: 10 minutes / **Cook time:** 10 minutes

Fruits and vegetables are not the only sources of antioxidants. Spices provide some antioxidants while adding flavor to a dish without adding sodium and fat. When the spices are combined with the omega-3 content of the salmon in this recipe, you've got an anti-inflammatory powerhouse.

½ tablespoon dried
  oregano
1 teaspoon sea salt
1 teaspoon garlic
  powder
½ teaspoon smoked
  paprika
½ teaspoon ground
  cumin
½ teaspoon dried thyme
¼ teaspoon freshly
  ground black pepper
¼ teaspoon cayenne
  pepper
4 (5-ounce) skin-on
  salmon fillets
1 tablespoon
  extra-virgin olive oil

1. In a small bowl, mix the oregano, salt, garlic powder, paprika, cumin, thyme, pepper, and cayenne.

2. Sprinkle the seasoning mix all over the salmon except the side with the skin.

3. Heat the oil in a large skillet over medium heat. Fry the fish for 3 minutes skin-side up, flip, and fry 3 minutes skin-side down until cooked through.

4. Serve.

5. Refrigerate leftovers in an airtight container for up to 2 days.

Serving Tip: Pair with Black Forbidden Rice with Bell Peppers (see page 107) or another favorite side.

Per serving (4 ounces): Calories 243; Fat: 12g; Carbohydrates: 1g; Fiber: 0g; Sugar: 0g; Protein: 31g; Sodium: 357mg

Mediterranean Chicken with Artichokes and Olives

Makes 4 servings
Prep time: 10 minutes / **Cook time:** 15 minutes

This chicken can be made in one pan, making it easy to prepare and cutting down on the number of dirty dishes in your sink. I love Mediterranean flavors, and the Mediterranean diet is consistently ranked as the healthiest diet by *US News and World Report*. Enjoy with Flavorful Farro (see page 108) or your favorite side.

1 pound chicken breast tenders (unbreaded)
½ teaspoon sea salt
⅛ teaspoon freshly ground black pepper
1 tablespoon extra-virgin olive oil, divided
1 small red onion, cut into very thin strips
1 teaspoon minced garlic
2 (14-ounce) cans artichoke hearts, drained and halved
¾ cup kalamata olives, pitted and halved
6 cups baby spinach leaves
1 cup basil leaves, julienned
½ cup shredded parmesan cheese

1. Season the breast tenders with the salt and pepper.

2. Heat ½ tablespoon of oil over medium-high heat in a large skillet. Add the tenders and cook each side for 2 minutes. Transfer the tenders to a plate with tongs and set the plate aside.

3. Using the same skillet, heat the remaining ½ tablespoon of oil over medium heat and sauté the onion and garlic for about 4 minutes, or until translucent.

4. Add the artichokes and olives and sauté for 4 minutes. Add half of the spinach and cook for about 1 minute; add the remaining spinach and cook for 1 minute, or until it wilts.

5. Add the basil and cook for 2 minutes. Add the chicken back to the skillet, cover, and cook for 2 minutes until heated through. Add the parmesan, mix well, and serve.

6. Refrigerate leftovers in an airtight container for up to 5 days.

Per serving (1½ cups): Calories 330; Fat: 12g; Carbohydrates: 24g; Fiber: 14g; Sugar: 2g; Protein: 35g; Sodium: 736mg

High-Protein Spaghetti with Creamy Butternut Squash Sauce

Making 6 servings
Prep time: 10 minutes / **Cook time:** 25 minutes

Pasta dishes are typically high in calories. We're using a high-protein, high-fiber pasta in this recipe, which is lower in calories than your typical pasta dish. This pasta choice has the added benefit of keeping you fuller for longer and regulating your blood glucose better. I recommend buying dried pasta that provides 5 grams or more of fiber and 10 grams or more of protein per serving.

20 ounces cubed butternut squash

1½ tablespoons extra-virgin olive oil, divided

1 teaspoon sea salt, divided

8 ounces high-fiber, high-protein spaghetti

1 medium onion, diced

1 teaspoon minced garlic

2 cups 1 percent milk

2 cups frozen broccoli florets, thawed

1 cup shredded cheddar cheese

½ cup shredded parmesan cheese

¼ teaspoon freshly ground black pepper

1. Preheat the oven to 450°F. Line a large baking sheet with aluminum foil.

2. Arrange the butternut squash in a single layer on the baking sheet, drizzle with ¾ tablespoon of oil, and sprinkle with ½ teaspoon of salt. Mix well using your hands, spread the squash out, and roast it for 20 minutes, or until slightly browned.

3. In the meantime, bring a large pot of water to a boil over high heat. Cook the pasta according to package instructions until al dente, about 10 minutes. Drain and set aside.

4. Heat the remaining ¾ tablespoon of oil in a large skillet over high heat and sauté the onion and garlic for 4 minutes until translucent.

5. Add the roasted butternut squash, onion mixture, and milk to a blender and blend until smooth.

6. Pour the butternut puree into a large pot over low-medium heat. Add the broccoli, cheddar cheese, parmesan cheese, remaining ½ teaspoon of salt, and pepper, and cook for 3 minutes until the cheese melts and the consistency is creamy.

7. Add the pasta to the pot, toss to combine, and serve.

8. Refrigerate leftovers in an airtight container for up to 5 days.

Variation Tip: Don't be shy with the veggies! Get creative and add your favorite non-starchy vegetables, such as Brussels sprouts, cauliflower, or zucchini.

Per serving (1 cup): Calories 380; Fat: 14g; Carbohydrates: 49g; Fiber: 5g; Sugar: 9g; Protein: 17g; Sodium: 521mg

Fusilli with Salmon and Lemon Caper Sauce

Makes 6 servings
Prep time: 10 minutes / **Cook time:** 35 minutes

You don't always have to enjoy salmon baked as a fillet. It can also be flaked and added to pasta, casseroles, or soups. Think of this recipe as an extra-delicious, high-end tuna casserole.

8 ounces high-fiber, high-protein fusilli pasta

Nonstick cooking spray

1 pound skinless salmon fillet

1 teaspoon sea salt, divided

1 tablespoon extra-virgin olive oil

1 small yellow or red onion, sliced

1 tablespoon minced garlic

1 pound frozen broccoli florets, thawed

1½ cup Greek yogurt, 2 percent, plain

¾ cup low-sodium chicken broth

3 tablespoons freshly squeezed lemon juice

1 tablespoon mustard

1 tablespoon capers

¼ teaspoon freshly ground black pepper

¼ cup chopped fresh parsley

1. Bring a large pot of water to a boil over high heat. Cook the pasta according to package instructions until al dente, about 12 minutes. Drain and set aside.

2. Preheat the oven to 400°F. Cover a baking sheet with foil and spray it with nonstick cooking spray.

3. Place the salmon on the baking sheet and sprinkle with ½ teaspoon of salt.

4. Bake for 12 minutes, or until the fish flakes when pressed with a fork. Cut the salmon into 2-inch cubes and set aside.

5. Heat the oil in a medium skillet over medium-high heat. Sauté the onion and garlic for about 3 minutes until softened.

6. Add the broccoli, yogurt, broth, lemon juice, mustard, capers, remaining ½ teaspoon of salt, and pepper, and cook for 5 minutes until warmed through.

7. Add the fusilli, salmon, and parsley and cook for another 2 minutes, tossing to combine.

8. Serve.

9. Refrigerate leftovers in an airtight container for up to 3 days.

Substitution Tip: You can use 16 ounces of canned salmon if you don't have the time to bake fresh salmon. Canned salmon also tends to be a bit more budget-friendly.

Per serving (1¼ cups): Calories 334; Fat: 9g; Carbohydrates: 39g; Fiber: 6g; Sugar: 6g; Protein: 28g; Sodium: 352mg

Vegetable Beef Stew with Cilantro

Makes 4 servings
Prep time: 7 minutes / **Cook time:** 1 hour

This stew is inspired by *seco,* one of the most common and beloved dishes in Peru. Even though it takes a little longer to make, the flavors that come together are worth it. It provides the right balance of potatoes, meat, and vegetables, so it is a prediabetes-friendly dish.

1 tablespoon extra-virgin olive oil

1 small red onion, diced

1 teaspoon minced garlic

1 pound beef stewing meat, cut into 1-inch pieces

1 bunch cilantro, coarsely chopped

1½ cups low-sodium beef broth

1½ teaspoons sea salt

1 teaspoon ground cumin

¼ teaspoon freshly ground black pepper

½ pound small yellow potatoes, halved

4 cups frozen mixed vegetables (peas, corn, carrots, green beans), thawed

1. Heat the oil over medium heat in a 4-quart stockpot, then sauté the onion and garlic for about 4 minutes, or until translucent.

2. Increase the heat to high, add the beef, cilantro, broth, salt, cumin, and pepper. Bring to a boil, cover, reduce the heat to low, and simmer for 25 minutes.

3. Add the potatoes and mixed vegetables to the stockpot and cook for another 20 minutes, or until the potatoes are soft. Mash about half the potatoes, stir, and cook for another 10 minutes.

4. Serve warm.

5. Refrigerate leftovers in an airtight container for up to 5 days.

Meal Prep Tip: Make this over the weekend so you can have a delicious stew during your busy work weekdays.

Per serving (1½ cups): Calories: 343; Fat: 8g; Carbohydrates: 36g; Fiber: 10g; Sugar: 7g ; Protein: 32g; Sodium: 599mg

Ground Chicken with Pinto Beans Picadillo

Makes 4 servings
Prep time: 10 minutes / **Cook time:** 25 minutes

I grew up with picadillo, a traditional Latin dish that reminds me of home. I wanted to share it with you. Using frozen and canned vegetables makes this a quick dinner recipe packed with nutrition and flavor.

1 tablespoon extra-virgin olive oil
1 medium red onion, diced
1 tablespoon minced garlic
2 zucchini, diced
3 celery stalks, diced
1 jalapeño pepper, seeded and diced

1 (15½-ounce) can low-sodium pinto beans, drained and rinsed
1 (14.5-ounce) can low-sodium diced tomatoes
1 pound ground chicken

2 cups mixed frozen vegetables (peas, carrots, green beans, and corn), thawed
2 teaspoons sea salt
1 teaspoon ground cumin
¼ teaspoon freshly ground black pepper
½ cup chopped fresh cilantro

1. Heat the oil in a medium skillet over medium-high heat. Sauté the onion and garlic for about 3 minutes until softened.

2. Reduce the heat to medium and add the zucchini, celery, and jalapeño and sauté for 8 minutes.

3. Add the beans and tomatoes and mix well. Add the ground chicken, veggies, salt, cumin, and pepper, cover, and cook for 10 minutes until the chicken is cooked through.

4. Add the cilantro, toss to combine, and serve.

5. Refrigerate leftovers in an airtight container for up to 4 days.

Substitution Tip: You can use lean ground turkey if you can't find ground chicken.

Per serving (2 cups): Calories 374; Fat: 14g; Carbohydrates: 36g; Fiber: 12g; Sugar: 7g; Protein: 31g; Sodium: 737mg

Creamy Vegetable Soup

Makes 5 servings
Prep time: 10 minutes / **Cook time:** 25 minutes

The inspiration for this dish was rich and creamy European milk soup intended to feed workers using just milk and potatoes. This adaptation is my answer to how to add more veggies to the original recipe to make it a more nutritious, heartier meal.

2 tablespoons extra-virgin olive oil

1 medium yellow onion, diced

1 teaspoon minced garlic

1 cup low-sodium chicken broth

10 ounces cremini mushrooms, sliced

8 ounces red potatoes, cubed

10 ounces broccoli florets

2 celery stalks, sliced

2 cups mixed frozen vegetables (corn, carrots, peas, and green beans)

3 cups 1 percent milk

1 cup shredded cheddar cheese

1 cup shredded parmesan cheese

2 teaspoons sea salt

¼ teaspoon freshly ground black pepper

1. In a large pot, heat the oil over medium heat and sauté the onion and garlic for 3 minutes until softened.

2. Add the broth, mushrooms, potatoes, broccoli, celery, and frozen vegetables and bring to a boil. Reduce the heat to low and simmer for 15 minutes, or until the vegetables are soft.

3. Add the milk, cheddar cheese, and parmesan cheese and simmer for 3 minutes, stirring, until the cheeses melt and the soup is creamy.

4. Season with the salt and pepper and serve.

5. Refrigerate leftovers in an airtight container for up to 5 days or freeze for 1 month.

Cooking Tip: This is a great way to use leftover vegetables in your refrigerator that are nearing the end of their shelf life.

Per serving (2 cups): Calories 407; Fat: 21g; Carbohydrates: 36g; Fiber: 6g; Sugar: 13g; Protein: 22g; Sodium: 1,098mg

Snacks and Treats

Low-Carb Quesadilla

Makes 1 serving
Prep time: 5 minutes / **Cook time:** 5 minutes

Who wouldn't like a cheesy quesadilla for a snack? These quesadillas are a great savory pick-me-up to tide you over in the afternoon until dinner and come together quickly and easily when hunger strikes.

1 (8-inch) low-carb
  tortilla
2 ounces part-skim
  shredded mozzarella

1. Heat a large skillet over medium heat.

2. Sprinkle the cheese on 1/2 of the tortilla and fold the other half over the cheese, pressing down.

3. Carefully place the folded tortilla in the skillet and cook for 2 minutes per side until the tortilla is golden brown and the cheese has melted.

Ingredient Tip: When choosing a low-carb tortilla, make sure to select one with no more than 10 grams of total carbohydrates and at least 3 grams of fiber.

Per serving (1 quesadilla): Calories 214; Fat: 12g; Carbohydrates: 21g; Fiber: 15g; Sugar: 1g; Protein: 19g; Sodium: 670mg

Avocado-Yogurt Dressing

Makes 4 servings
Prep time: 10 minutes

This is a versatile dressing for salads and a topping for meats or poultry. Yogurt contains good bacteria that keep your gut healthy, and avocado is rich in prebiotic fiber to feed these bacteria to keep them active and multiplying.

1 medium ripe avocado, peeled, pitted, and cubed

1 tablespoon freshly squeezed lime juice

½ cup plain 2 percent Greek yogurt

½ cup chopped tomatoes

1 jalapeño pepper, seeded and diced

2 tablespoons chopped red onion

1 tablespoon chopped fresh cilantro

½ teaspoon sea salt

¼ teaspoon freshly ground black pepper

1. In a medium bowl, mash the avocado and lime juice with a fork until it reaches your desired consistency.

2. Add the Greek yogurt, tomatoes, jalapeño, onion, and cilantro and mix well.

3. Taste and season with the salt and pepper. Serve.

4. Refrigerate leftovers in an airtight container for up to 3 days.

Serving Tip: You can also dip raw vegetables in this yummy dressing.

Per serving (½ cup): Calories 111; Fat: 8g; Carbohydrates: 9g; Fiber: 4g; Sugar: 4g; Protein: 3g; Sodium: 173mg

Egg Salad Veggie Cups

Makes 4 servings
Prep time: 15 minutes / **Cook time:** 10 minutes

Due to the eggs and yogurt, this is a high-protein snack that can help control appetite and blood glucose. The addition of apple provides soluble fiber to help you feel full longer.

4 large eggs
1 celery stalk, finely chopped
½ cup finely diced red bell pepper
½ cup diced Honeycrisp apple
½ cup 2 percent plain Greek yogurt
¼ cup finely diced yellow onion
1 tablespoon yellow mustard
½ tablespoon extra-virgin olive oil
½ teaspoon sea salt
½ teaspoon freshly ground black pepper
8 butterhead lettuce leaves

1. Place the eggs in a single layer in a small saucepan and cover them with cold water. Bring to a boil over high heat and boil for 7 minutes. Take the saucepan off the heat, drain the eggs, and place them immediately in a bowl of ice water. Peel and chop the eggs once they are cool.

2. In a large bowl, mix the chopped eggs, celery, bell pepper, apple, yogurt, onion, mustard, oil, salt, and pepper until well combined.

3. Layer two lettuce leaves together and place ½ cup of the salad in the middle. Fold in half like a taco. Repeat with the remaining leaves and salad.

4. Refrigerate leftover egg salad and lettuce separately in an airtight container for up to 3 days. Load the cups when ready to eat.

Serving Tip: If you decide to bring this snack to work, separate the egg salad from the lettuce and load the cups right before eating to prevent wilting.

Per serving (2 lettuce leaves and ½ cup salad): Calories 130; Fat: 7g; Carbohydrates: 7g; Fiber: 1g; Sugar: 5g; Protein: 9g; Sodium: 432mg

Roast Beef and Vegetable Rolls

Makes 4 servings
Prep time: 5 minutes / **Cook time:** 5 minutes

You might not know that roast beef is a lean meat that is lower in saturated fat than other cuts of meat. This leanness keeps the calories low and ensures that this dish is heart-healthy.

1 teaspoon extra-virgin olive oil

1 small red bell pepper, seeded and cut into thin strips

1 zucchini, cut into thin strips

1 tablespoon store-bought balsamic glaze

8 (1-ounce) slices roast beef

8 fresh basil leaves

1. Heat the oil in a large skillet over medium heat and sauté the bell pepper and zucchini for about 4 minutes, until softened.

2. Add the balsamic glaze and cook for 1 minute. Remove from the heat and set aside.

3. Layer together 2 slices of roast beef and top with 2 basil leaves and ¼ of the vegetables. Roll the roast beef in a tight roll and serve.

4. Refrigerate leftovers in an airtight container for up to 4 days.

Substitution Tip: Other lean meats like chicken or turkey can be used in place of the beef.

Per serving (1 beef roll): Calories 132; Fat: 6g; Carbohydrates: 3g; Fiber: 1g; Sugar: 3g; Protein: 16g; Sodium: 51mg

Roasted Spiced Chickpeas

Makes 6 servings
Prep time: 5 minutes / **Cook time:** 35 minutes

Roasted chickpeas can be a surprisingly indulgent treat. They contain a starch called amylose that digests slowly, which is great for blood glucose control. Also, turmeric adds an anti-inflammatory kick.

2 (15½-ounce) cans chickpeas, drained, rinsed, and thoroughly dried

2 teaspoons curry powder

1 teaspoon sea salt

¼ teaspoon ground cumin

¼ teaspoon turmeric

¼ teaspoon garlic powder

¼ teaspoon freshly ground black pepper

1 tablespoon extra-virgin olive oil

1. Preheat the oven to 400°F.

2. Spread the chickpeas on a baking sheet and dry them in the oven for 25 minutes.

3. While the chickpeas are drying, in a medium bowl, mix the curry powder, salt, cumin, turmeric, garlic powder, and pepper.

4. Once the chickpeas are completely dry, drizzle them with the oil, sprinkle with the spice mixture, and toss to coat.

5. Spread the chickpeas out evenly again and roast for 5 to 10 minutes until browned and crisp.

6. Store the chickpeas in an airtight container at room temperature for up to 5 days.

Meal Prep Tip: These are the perfect make-ahead, high-fiber, savory snack to hold you over between main meals.

Per serving (¼ cup): Calories 158; Fat: 4g; Carbohydrates: 23g; Fiber: 7g; Sugar: 4g; Protein: 7g; Sodium: 200mg

Cottage Cheese Parfait

Makes 1 serving
Prep time: 5 minutes

Move aside, Greek yogurt! Nowadays, more and more cottage cheese brands include probiotics. If you want to switch up your dairy delights, go for some cottage cheese—which is higher in protein per serving than Greek yogurt.

½ cup 2 percent cultured small curd cottage cheese
¾ cup fresh berries of choice
1 teaspoon honey
½ teaspoon ground cinnamon
1 tablespoon chopped walnuts

1. Spoon the cottage cheese into a small glass container.

2. Layer the berries on top of the yogurt, drizzle with the honey, sprinkle with the cinnamon, and top with the walnuts before enjoying.

Meal Prep Tip: You can make several of these in advance in little jars. They can last for up to 4 days in the refrigerator.

Per serving (1 parfait): Calories 228; Fat: 8g; Carbohydrates: 29g; Fiber: 4g; Sugar: 22g; Protein: 14g; Sodium: 350mg

High-Protein Pumpkin-Chia Pudding

Makes 2 servings
Prep time: 5 minutes, plus 4 hours to chill

Pumpkin is a low-carb starchy vegetable that adds a lot of fun flavor. This high-protein recipe can double as both a delicious breakfast option and a satisfying dessert.

1 cup pumpkin puree
1 cup 1 percent milk
½ cup 2 percent plain Greek yogurt
3 tablespoons chia seeds
1 tablespoon pure vanilla extract
½ tablespoon ground cinnamon
1 teaspoon honey
Pinch sea salt

1. In a medium container with a lid, mix the pumpkin puree, milk, yogurt, chia seeds, vanilla, cinnamon, honey, and salt until well blended.

2. Cover and refrigerate for at least 4 hours or overnight before enjoying.

3. Refrigerate leftovers in an airtight container for up to 4 days.

Ingredient Tip: If you don't want to waste your extra canned pumpkin, double the recipe and store the excess in jars in the refrigerator to grab when you're ready to enjoy them.

Per serving (1 cup): Calories 269; Fat: 9g; Carbohydrates: 35g; Fiber: 12g; Sugar: 18g; Protein: 12g; Sodium: 185mg

Cacao Mousse

Makes 4 servings
Prep time: 10 minutes, plus 4 hours to chill

This is the recipe for you if you are a chocolate lover. This dessert is not overly sweet but can satisfy the sweet tooth or chocolate craving you may experience between meals.

1 (8-ounce) container low-fat cream cheese, at room temperature
5 tablespoons 1 percent milk
¼ cup cacao powder
2 tablespoons monk fruit sweetener
½ tablespoon pure vanilla extract
1 teaspoon ground cinnamon
Pinch sea salt

1. Place the cream cheese, milk, cacao powder, sweetener, vanilla, cinnamon, and salt in a medium bowl. Beat until combined with handheld electric beaters on medium speed.

2. Cover with plastic wrap and chill in the refrigerator for 4 hours before enjoying.

3. Refrigerate leftovers in an airtight container for up to 3 days.

Serving Tip: Eat this one mindfully because the calories can add up fast.

Per serving (3 fluid ounces): Calories 140; Fat: 10g; Carbohydrates: 9g; Fiber: 2g; Sugar: 5g; Protein: 6g; Sodium: 252mg

High-Protein Mango Mousse

Makes 2 servings
Prep time: 10 minutes

This mousse comes out so creamy that you'll think you made ice cream. Even though mangos are sweet, they have a low glycemic index of 50, making them diabetic-safe. Studies have shown that regular consumption of mangos can reduce blood glucose in both men and women. In addition to reducing blood sugar, consumption of mangos can aid in reducing waist size, which is critical to helping improve insulin resistance.

2 tablespoons 1 percent milk
1 cup frozen mango
½ cup plain 2 percent Greek yogurt
1 scoop vanilla protein powder (whey, soy, pea, or rice, with at least 20 grams of protein per serving)

1. Pour the milk into a high-speed blender; then add the mango, yogurt, and protein powder.

2. Blend until smooth, pour into a bowl, and enjoy.

Serving Tip: Enjoy as a dessert or as a post-workout treat because the inclusion of fast-absorbing whey protein is helpful for muscle recovery.

Per serving (¾ cup): Calories 147; Fat 2g; Carbohydrates: 22g; Fiber: 1g; Sugar: 16g; Protein: 13g; Sodium: 104mg

Apple-Pineapple Bake

Makes 4 servings
Prep time: 10 minutes / **Cook time:** 35 minutes

Are you an apple pie fan? Well, you're going to love this recipe. The warm flavors of the apple and cinnamon make it a perfect treat for a chilly night.

Nonstick cooking spray
¼ cup light butter, melted
½ tablespoon pure vanilla extract
3 tablespoons monk fruit sweetener
1 tablespoon ground cinnamon
½ teaspoon ground nutmeg
⅛ teaspoon sea salt
1 pound sliced Honeycrisp apples
1 cup canned pineapple chunks in 100 percent pineapple juice, drained
½ cup chopped pecans

1. Preheat the oven to 375°F. Coat an 11-by-8-inch baking dish with nonstick cooking spray and set aside.

2. In a small bowl, mix the butter and vanilla.

3. In another small bowl, mix the sweetener, cinnamon, nutmeg, and salt.

4. Place the apples and pineapple in the prepared baking dish, tossing to combine. Sprinkle the pecans all over the fruit.

5. Drizzle the butter mixture all over the fruit and sprinkle evenly with the sweetener mixture.

6. Bake uncovered for 35 minutes until lightly browned and bubbly. Serve warm.

7. Refrigerate leftovers in an airtight container for up to 5 days.

Serving Tip: Serve a portion of this baked fruit over Greek yogurt for a delicious treat. It's a great way to add protein to the recipe for glucose control.

Per serving (1 cup): Calories: 257; Fat: 18g; Carbohydrates: 25g; Fiber: 6g; Sugar: 17g; Protein: 2g; Sodium: 104mg

Peanut Butter–Cacao Balls

Makes 6 servings
Prep time: 5 minutes

For those looking for a sweet, preworkout energy treat, this is a great one to try. It is fun to make and so indulgent, you will feel like you're eating candy without the sugar rush.

1 cup peanut butter or almond butter

2 tablespoons cacao nibs

1 tablespoon honey

1 tablespoon chia seeds

1 tablespoon cacao powder

2 tablespoons psyllium husk

1 scoop chocolate protein powder (whey, soy, pea, or rice with 25 grams protein per serving)

1. In a large bowl, combine the peanut butter, cacao nibs, honey, chia seeds, and cacao powder.

2. Add the psyllium husk and protein powder and mix well. When the mixture starts looking dry, start kneading with your hands to form a dough.

3. Divide the dough into 12 equal balls (1 ounce or 2 tablespoons per ball) and enjoy!

4. Refrigerate leftovers in an airtight container for up to 1 week.

Substitution Tip: Nut allergy? Use the same amount of sunflower seed butter instead of nut butter.

Per serving (2 balls): Calories 310; Fat: 24g; Carbohydrates: 16g; Fiber: 4g; Sugar: 7g; Protein: 13g; Sodium: 26mg

Golden Milk with Cacao

Makes 1 serving
Prep time: 5 minutes / **Cook time:** 5 minutes

Sometimes, you want to end your night with something comforting after a long day. Unfortunately, drinks like hot chocolate can spike blood sugar quickly, but this substitute with antioxidants from turmeric and cacao can be enjoyed safely before bed.

1 cup 1 percent milk
1 teaspoon honey
1 tablespoon cacao powder
¼ teaspoon ground turmeric
¼ teaspoon ground cinnamon
Freshly ground black pepper

1. In a small saucepan, gently heat the milk with honey over medium heat. Stir occasionally and bring to almost boiling with small bubbles forming around the edge of the pan, 2 to 3 minutes.

2. Remove the saucepan from the heat and whisk in the cacao powder, turmeric, and cinnamon until well blended. Let the mixture stand for 2 minutes. Add a sprinkle of pepper and enjoy.

Serving Tip: Double the recipe if you want to share this warming treat with a friend or partner.

Per serving (1 cup): Calories 140: Fat: 3g; Carbohydrates: 22g; Fiber: 2g; Sugar: 19g; Protein: 9g; Sodium: 109mg

CHAPTER 6

Homemade Staples and Sides

Sheet Pan Roasted Vegetables

Makes 6 servings
Prep time: 10 minutes / **Cook time:** 20 minutes

This recipe converted many of my clients into vegetable believers, even if they hated eating them before. Roasting is quick with minimal cleanup. This cooking method brings out the natural, rich flavors of the vegetables, making them the perfect side to almost any meal.

Nonstick cooking spray

1 head cauliflower, cut into small florets

1 medium red onion, cut into 1-inch pieces

1 medium bell pepper (any color), seeded and cut into 1-inch chunks

1 zucchini, cut into 1-inch pieces

1 carrot, cut into 1-inch pieces

2 cups halved Brussels sprouts

1 tablespoon extra-virgin olive oil

1½ teaspoons sea salt

½ teaspoon freshly ground black pepper

1. Preheat the oven to 450°F. Line a baking sheet with foil and spray it with nonstick cooking spray.

2. In a large bowl, toss the cauliflower, onion, bell pepper, zucchini, carrot, Brussels sprouts, oil, salt, and pepper until well coated.

3. Spread the vegetables on the baking sheet in a single layer and roast for 20 minutes, or until they are tender and their edges are brown.

4. Refrigerate leftovers in an airtight container for up to 3 days.

Variation Tip: After the third day, put the wilting veggies in a blender with some broth to make a tasty, blended vegetable soup.

Per serving (1½ cups): Calories: 67; Fat: 3g; Carbohydrates: 10g; Fiber: 3g; Sugar: 4g; Protein: 3g; Sodium: 322mg

Butternut Squash, Carrot, and Sweet Potato Fries

Makes 6 servings
Prep time: 10 minutes / **Cook time:** 20 minutes

These fries can be paired with pretty much anything you'd eat regular French fries with: sandwiches, burgers, or even steak. Unlike your traditional fast-food fries, the best part is that these are higher in fiber and antioxidants, making them more prediabetes-friendly.

Nonstick cooking spray
8 ounces butternut squash, cut into 4-by-½-inch strips
8 ounces sweet potato, peeled and cut into 4-by-½-inch strips
8 ounces carrot, cut into 4-by-½-inch strips
1 tablespoon extra-virgin olive oil
1 teaspoon sea salt

1. Preheat the oven to 450°F. Line a baking sheet with foil and spray it with nonstick cooking spray.

2. In a large bowl, toss the squash, sweet potato, carrot, oil, and salt until well coated.

3. Spread the fries in a single layer on the baking sheet and roast for 20 minutes, or until they are tender and their edges are brown.

4. Refrigerate leftovers in an airtight container for up to 2 days.

Serving Tip: For the best results, consume these the same day. If reheating, heat in a 350°F oven for 15 minutes until crispy. Do not use the microwave.

Per serving (175 grams of vegetables): Calories: 82; Fat: 2g; Carbohydrates: 15g; Fiber: 3g; Sugar: 3g; Protein: 1g; Sodium: 224mg

Steamed Broccoli and Cauliflower with Lemon

Makes 4 servings
Prep time: 10 minutes / **Cook time:** 5 minutes

What a delicious way to get your cruciferous vegetables! And it's ready in about 15 minutes. The simple seasoning of lemon and sea salt enhances the flavors without the added calories of sauces and unhealthy fats.

½ head (3½ cups)
broccoli florets
½ head (3½ cups)
cauliflower florets
2 tablespoons freshly
squeezed lemon juice
1 tablespoon
extra-virgin olive oil
½ teaspoon sea salt

ON THE STOVETOP

1. Place 1 to 2 inches of water in the bottom of a large saucepan with a lid and heat over high heat until boiling. Add the broccoli and cauliflower and cover.

2. Cook for 3 to 4 minutes, or until semi-soft. Transfer the vegetables to a colander (strainer) and run cold water over them.

3. Transfer the vegetables to a serving bowl and toss with the lemon juice, oil, and salt.

4. Serve or refrigerate in an airtight container for up to 2 days.

IN THE MICROWAVE

1. Wash the broccoli and cauliflower, place them in a large microwave-safe bowl, and loosely cover with a lid or a microwave cover.

2. Microwave for 3 to 4 minutes, or until the desired tenderness is reached.

3. Transfer the vegetables to a colander (strainer) and run cold water over them.

4. Transfer the vegetables to a serving bowl and toss with the lemon juice, oil, and salt.

5. Serve or refrigerate in an airtight container for up to 2 days.

Serving Tip: This is a great recipe to snack on while cooking dinner. Since the calories are low, you will curb your appetite without sabotaging your eating plan.

Per serving (1½ cups): Calories: 76; Fat: 4g; Carbohydrates: 9g; Fiber: 4g; Sugar: 3g; Protein: 4g; Sodium: 193mg

Greek-Inspired Roasted Chicken Breast

Makes 4 servings
Prep time: 15 minutes / **Cook time:** 15 minutes

What is the first word that typically comes to mind when you think of poorly prepared chicken breast? Dry. This chicken breast comes out juicy and flavorful every time. It all has to do with timing, temperature, and the cut of the chicken. Greek seasonings also add flavor.

Nonstick cooking spray
1 pound boneless,
  skinless chicken
  breasts
2 tablespoons freshly
  squeezed lemon juice
1 tablespoon
  extra-virgin olive oil
1 tablespoon dried
  oregano
1 teaspoon sea salt
½ teaspoon garlic
  powder
½ teaspoon freshly
  ground black pepper

1. Preheat the oven to 500°F. Spray a 9-by-13-inch baking dish with nonstick cooking spray.

2. Butterfly the chicken on a cutting board by placing your hand on top of the breast and using a chef's knife to slice into one side of the breast, starting at the thicker end and ending at the thin point. Be careful not to cut all the way through to the other side.

3. In a large bowl, toss the chicken, lemon juice, oil, oregano, salt, garlic powder, and pepper.

4. Place the chicken breasts with the sides folded out like a butterfly in a single layer in the prepared baking dish and bake for 12 minutes, until cooked through.

5. Remove the chicken from the oven and let it sit for 5 minutes.

6. Serve. Refrigerate leftovers in an airtight container for up to 5 days.

Meal Prep Tip: Cook this chicken in bulk to add to other recipes throughout this book for the week. This preparation will cut down drastically on your meal prep time.

Per serving (3 ounces): Calories: 159; Fat: 5g; Carbohydrates: 1g; Fiber: 0g; Sugar: 0g; Protein: 25g; Sodium: 349mg

Baked Salmon with Balsamic Glaze

Makes 4 servings
Prep time: 10 minutes **/ Cook time:** 15 minutes

It seems not all are fans of fish, but fatty fish like salmon contain an anti-oxidant we need to fight visceral fat. Omega-3s are essential for our brain and heart health, and we can only get them from food or supplements. This oven-baked salmon recipe is a delicious way to get this necessary nutrient.

Nonstick cooking spray
1 pound boneless, skinless salmon fillets
½ teaspoon sea salt
¼ teaspoon freshly ground black pepper
¼ teaspoon garlic powder
1 tablespoon store-bought balsamic glaze

1. Preheat the oven to 450°F. Line a baking sheet with foil and spray with nonstick cooking spray.

2. Place the salmon on the baking sheet and sprinkle with the salt, pepper, and garlic powder.

3. Spread the glaze over the salmon, making sure to cover the top of the fish.

4. Bake for 12 minutes, or until the fish flakes when pressed with a fork.

5. Serve or refrigerate in an airtight container for up to 3 days.

Serving Tip: Add this salmon to recipes like the Gut Healthy Chopped Salad (see page 60) to make a complete meal, or substitutue it for chicken in the Pico de Gallo, Black Bean, and Chicken Bowl (see page 72).

Per serving (3 ounces salmon): Calories: 208; Fat: 12g; Carbohydrates: 1g; Fiber: 0g; Sugar: 1g; Protein: 23g; Sodium: 200mg

Roasted Small Tricolored Potatoes

Makes 4 servings
Prep time: 10 minutes / **Cook time:** 25 minutes

Contrary to popular belief, potatoes are not your enemy when controlling weight, especially when they come in different colors. The different colors represent different antioxidants that can help regulate glucose and fight inflammation. Add that to the spices, and this recipe is an antioxidant powerhouse.

Nonstick cooking spray

1½ pounds tricolored potatoes, halved

1 tablespoon dried oregano

1 tablespoon extra-virgin olive oil

½ tablespoon paprika

1 teaspoon garlic powder

1 teaspoon sea salt

¼ teaspoon freshly ground black pepper

1. Preheat the oven to 400°F. Line a baking sheet with foil and spray it with nonstick cooking spray.

2. In a large bowl, toss the potatoes, oregano, oil, paprika, garlic powder, salt, and pepper until well coated.

3. Spread the potatoes on the baking sheet in a single layer and roast for 25 minutes, or until they are tender and their edges are brown.

4. Refrigerate leftovers in an airtight container for up to 3 days and add to your meals as desired.

Ingredient Tip: If you can't find tricolored potatoes, you can use whatever small potatoes are available in your grocery store. You can also use fresh chives in place of the dried oregano, if preferred.

Per serving (1¼ cup or 175 grams): Calories: 168; Fat: 4g; Carbohydrates: 31g; Fiber: 4g; Sugar: 1g; Protein: 4g; Sodium: 302mg

Black Forbidden Rice with Bell Peppers

Makes 8 servings
Prep time: 10 minutes / **Cook time:** 50 minutes

Compared to white or brown rice, black rice is top tier in fiber and protein and is available in most grocery stores or international markets. Calorie-wise, it may be about the same per serving as other rice, but the same serving size will help you feel fuller and control blood glucose better due to the anthocyanin content.

1 tablespoon extra-virgin olive oil
½ yellow onion, diced
1 cup diced red bell pepper
1 teaspoon minced garlic
4 cups low-sodium vegetable or chicken broth
2 cups black rice, rinsed
1 teaspoon sea salt

1. Heat the oil in a small saucepan over medium-high heat and sauté the onion for 3 minutes until softened. Add the bell pepper and garlic and sauté for 1 minute.

2. Add the broth, rice, and salt, and bring to a boil. Cover, reduce the heat to low, and simmer until the water has been absorbed, about 45 minutes.

3. Fluff the black rice with a fork and serve immediately or cool and refrigerate in an airtight container for up to 5 days.

Serving Tip: Use this in any other recipe in which you would usually use white or brown rice, including stir-fry, as a bed for your chicken or salmon, or even with breakfast underneath two fried eggs.

Per serving (¾ cup): Calories 196; Fat: 3g; Carbohydrates: 38g; Fiber: 2g; Sugar: 1g; Protein: 4g; Sodium: 148mg

Flavorful Farro

Makes 6 servings
Prep time: 5 minutes / **Cook time:** 45 minutes

Farro is an ancient grain and an excellent source of fiber and protein. This heart-healthy grain can replace rice or other grains in your dishes if you are looking for variety in the starch portion of your plate.

1 teaspoon extra-virgin olive oil

¼ cup diced yellow onion

¼ teaspoon minced garlic

3 cups water or low-sodium vegetable/chicken broth

1 cup farro, rinsed

½ teaspoon sea salt

1. Heat the oil in a small saucepan over medium-high heat and sauté the onion for 3 minutes until softened. Add the garlic and sauté for 1 minute.

2. Add the water, farro, and salt to the saucepan and bring to a boil. Cover, reduce the heat to low and simmer until the farro is soft, 35 to 40 minutes.

3. Strain the farro through a sieve to remove the excess water and transfer the solids to a bowl.

4. Fluff the farro with a fork and serve, or cool and refrigerate in an airtight container for up to 5 days.

Ingredient Tip: You can get precooked farro at the grocery store to cut down on preparation time. Just measure the serving size to match what is here to keep calories consistent.

Per serving (½ cup): Calories: 92; Fat: 1g; Carbohydrates: 17g; Fiber: 3g; Sugar: 0g; Protein: 3g; Sodium: 101mg

MEASUREMENT CONVERSIONS

VOLUME EQUIVALENTS	U.S. STANDARD	U.S. STANDARD (OUNCES)	METRIC (APPROXIMATE)
LIQUID	2 tablespoons	1 fl. oz.	30 mL
	¼ cup	2 fl. oz.	60 mL
	½ cup	4 fl. oz.	120 mL
	1 cup	8 fl. oz.	240 mL
	1½ cups	12 fl. oz.	355 mL
	2 cups or 1 pint	16 fl. oz.	475 mL
	4 cups or 1 quart	32 fl. oz.	1 L
	1 gallon	128 fl. oz.	4 L
DRY	⅛ teaspoon	–	0.5 mL
	¼ teaspoon	–	1 mL
	½ teaspoon	–	2 mL
	¾ teaspoon	–	4 mL
	1 teaspoon	–	5 mL
	1 tablespoon	–	15 mL
	¼ cup	–	59 mL
	⅓ cup	–	79 mL
	½ cup	–	118 mL
	⅔ cup	–	156 mL
	¾ cup	–	177 mL
	1 cup	–	235 mL
	2 cups or 1 pint	–	475 mL
	3 cups	–	700 mL
	4 cups or 1 quart	–	1 L
	½ gallon	–	2 L
	1 gallon	–	4 L

OVEN TEMPERATURES

FAHRENHEIT	CELSIUS (APPROXIMATE)
250°F	120°C
300°F	150°C
325°F	165°C
350°F	180°C
375°F	190°C
400°F	200°C
425°F	220°C
450°F	230°C

WEIGHT EQUIVALENTS

U.S. STANDARD	METRIC (APPROXIMATE)
½ ounce	15 g
1 ounce	30 g
2 ounces	60 g
4 ounces	115 g
8 ounces	225 g
12 ounces	340 g
16 ounces or 1 pound	455 g

REFERENCES

BLOOD GLUCOSE CONTROL AND INSULIN RESISTANCE

Biddinger, S. B., A. Hernandez-Ono, C. Rask-Madsen, et al. "Hepatic Insulin Resistance Is Sufficient to Produce Dyslipidemia and Susceptibility to Atherosclerosis." *Cell Metabolism* 7 (2008): 125–34.

Dubé, J. J., F. Amati, F. G. Toledo, et al. "Effects of Weight Loss and Exercise on Insulin Resistance, and Intramyocellular Triacylglycerol, Diacylglycerol and Ceramide." *Diabetologia* 54 (2011): 1147–56.

Gastaldelli, A., M. Gaggini, and R. A. DeFronzo. "Role of Adipose Tissue Insulin Resistance in the Natural History of Type 2 Diabetes: Results from the San Antonio Metabolism Study." *Diabetes* 66 (2017): 815–22.

Hu, W., C. Jiang, D. Guan, et al. "Patient Adipose Stem Cell-Derived Adipocytes Reveal Genetic Variation That Predicts Antidiabetic Drug Response." *Cell Stem Cell* 24 (2019): 299–308.

Manson, J. E., E. B. Rimm, M. J. Stampfer, G. A. Colditz, W. C. Willett, A. S. Krolewski, B. Rosner, C. H. Hennekens, and F. E. Speizer. "Physical Activity and Incidence of Non-Insulin-Dependent Diabetes Mellitus in Women." *Lancet* 338 (1991): 774–78.

National Center for Chronic Disease Prevention and Health Promotion. "Age-Specific Prevalence of Diagnosed Diabetes, by Race/Ethnicity and Sex, United States." 2004. CDC.gov/diabetes/statistics/prev/national/fig2004.htm.

Shimobayashi, M., V. Albert, B. Woelnerhanssen, et al. "Insulin Resistance Causes Inflammation in Adipose Tissue." *Journal of Clinical Investigation* 128 (2018): 1538–50.

Vijayakumar, A., P. Aryal, J. Wen, et al. "Absence of Carbohydrate Response Element Binding Protein in Adipocytes Causes Systemic Insulin Resistance and Impairs Glucose Transport." *Cell Reports* 21 (2017): 1021–35.

Westerbacka, J., A.Cornér, K. Kannisto, et al. "Acute In Vivo Effects of Insulin on Gene Expression in Adipose Tissue in Insulin-Resistant and Insulin-Sensitive Subjects." *Diabetologia* 49 (2006): 132–40.

Willett, W., M. J. Stampfer, C. Bain, R. Lipnick, F. E. Speizer, B. Rosner, D. Cramer, and C. H. Hennekens. "Cigarette Smoking, Relative Weight, and Menopause." *American Journal of Epidemiology* 117 (1983): 651–58.

GUT MICROBIOME AND WEIGHT/HEALTH

Bruce-Keller, Annadora J., J. Michael Salbaum, Meng Luo, et al. "Obese-Type Gut Microbiota Induce Neurobehavioral Changes in the Absence of Obesity." *Biological Psychiatry* 77 (2015): 607–15.

Byerley, L., D. Samuelson, E. Blanchard IV, et al. "Changes in the Gut Microbial Communities following Addition of Walnuts to the Diet." *The Journal of Nutritional Biochemistry* 48 (2017): 94–102.

De Filippo, C., D. Cavalieri, M. Di Paola, M. Ramazzotti, J. B. Poullet, S. Massart, et al. "Impact of Diet in Shaping Gut Microbiota Revealed by a Comparative Study in Children from Europe and Rural Africa." *Proceedings of the National Academy of Sciences of the United States of America* 107 (2010): 14691–96.

Delzenne, N. M., and P. D. Cani. "Interaction between Obesity and the Gut Microbiota: Relevance in Nutrition." *Annual Review of Nutrition* 31 (2011): 15–31.

Lu, K., R. Mahbub, and J. G. Fox. "Xenobiotics: Interaction with the Intestinal Microflora." *ILAR Journal* 56 (2015): 218–27.

INFLAMMATION AND VISCERAL FAT

Fontana, L. J. C., and M. Trujillo. "Visceral Fat Adipokine Secretion Is Associated with Systemic Inflammation in Obese Humans." *Diabetes* 56, no. 4 (2007): 1010–13.

Foster, M. T., H. Shi, R. J. Seeley, and S. C. Woods. Removal of Intra-Abdominal Visceral Adipose Tissue Improves Glucose Tolerance in Rats: Role of Hepatic Triglyceride Storage. *Physiology & Behavior* 104, no. 5 (2011): 845–54.

Hubertus, H., F. Stephany, L. Jakob, S. Henrike, W. Günther, H. Stephanie, G. Kurt, and P. Thomas. "TNF-α, Soluble TNF Receptor and Interleukin-6 Plasma Levels in the General Population." *European Cytokine Network* 17, no. 3 (2006): 196–201.

Manigrasso, M. R., P. Ferroni, et al. "Association between Circulating Adiponectin and Interleukin-10 Levels in Android Obesity: Effects of Weight Loss." *The Journal of Clinical Endocrinology & Metabolism* 90, no. 10 (2005): 5876–79.

Nam, S. Y., I. J. Choi, K. H. Ryu, B. J. Park, Y. W. Kim, H. B. Kim, and J. Kim. "The Effect of Abdominal Visceral Fat, Circulating Inflammatory Cytokines, and Leptin Levels." *Journal of Neurogastroenterology and Motility* 21, no. 2 (2015): 247–54.

Sang Wook, K. "Association between Visceral Fat and Inflammatory Cytokines.: *Journal of Neurogastroenterology and Motility* 21, no. 2: (2015): 145–46.

Schmidt, F. M., J. Weschenfelder, C. Sander, J. Minkwitz, J. Thormann, et al. "Inflammatory Cytokines in General and Central Obesity and Modulating Effects of Physical Activity." *PLOS One* 10, no. 3 (2015).

Suárez-Álvarez, K., L. Solís-Lozano, S. Leon-Cabrera, A. González-Chávez, G. Gómez-Hernández, M. S. Quiñones-Álvarez. "Serum IL-12 Is Increased in Mexican Obese Subjects and Associated with Low-Grade Inflammation and Obesity-Related Parameters." *Mediators of Inflammation* (2013): 967067.

Tateya, S., F. Kim, and Y. Tamori. "Recent Advances in Obesity-Induced Inflammation and Insulin Resistance." *Frontiers in Endocrinology* 4 (2013): 93.

Trayhurn, P., and I. Wood. "Adipokines: Inflammation and the Pleiotropic Role of White Adipose Tissue." *British Journal of Nutrition* 92, no. 3 (2004): 347–55.

MEAL FREQUENCY

Farshchi, H. R., M. A. Taylor, and I. A. Macdonald. "Regular Meal Frequency Creates More Appropriate Insulin Sensitivity and Lipid Profiles Compared with Irregular Meal Frequency in Healthy Lean Women." *European Journal of Clinical Nutrition* 58 (2004): 1071–77.

STRESS AND EATING/HEALTH

Anderson, D. A., et al. "Self-Reported Dietary Restraint Is Associated with Elevated Levels of Salivary Cortisol." *Appetite* 38 (2002): 13–17.

Block, J. P., et al. "Psychosocial Stress and Change in Weight among US Adults." *American Journal of Epidemiology* 170 (2009): 181–92.

Cameron, M. J., R. W. Maguire, and J. McCormack. "Stress-Induced Binge Eating: A Behavior Analytic Approach to Assessment and Intervention." *Journal of Adult Development* 18 (2001): 81–84.

George, S. A., et al. "CRH-Stimulated Cortisol Release and Food Intake in Healthy, Non-Obese Adults." *Psychoneuroendocrinology* 35 (2010): 607–12.

Kandiah, J., M. Yake, and H. Willett. "Effects of Stress on Eating Practices among Adults." *Family and Consumer Sciences Research Journal* 37, no. 1 (2008): 27–38.

Martens, M. J. I., et al. "Effects of Single Macronutrients on Serum Cortisol Concentrations in Normal Weight Men." *Physiology & Behavior* 101 (2010): 563–67.

Tomiyama, J., et al. "Low Calorie Dieting Increases Cortisol." *Psychosomatic Medicine* 72, no. 4 (2010): 357–64.

Torres, S. J., and C. A. Nowson. "Relationship between Stress, Eating Behavior, and Obesity." *Nutrition* 23 (2007): 887–94.

Vicennati, V., et al. "Cortisol, Energy Intake, and Food Frequency in Overweight/Obese Women." *Nutrition* 27 (2011): 677–80.

UNSATURATED FATS AND FAT LOSS

Farr, O., T. Dario, U. Jagriti, M. Sabrina, and M. Christos. "Walnut Consumption Increases Activation of the Insula to Highly Desirable Food Cues: A Randomized, Double-Blind, Placebo-Controlled, Cross-Over FMRI Study." *Journal of Pharmacology and Therapeutics* 20, no. 1 (2017): 173–77.

Neale, E. P., L. C. Tapsell, A. Martin, et al. "Impact of Providing Walnut Samples in a Lifestyle Intervention for Weight Loss: A Secondary Analysis of the HealthTrack Trial." *Food & Nutrition Research* 61, no. 1 (2017).

Tapsell, L. C., M. Lonergan, M. J. Batterham, et al. "Effect of Interdisciplinary Care on Weight Loss: A Randomised Controlled Trial." *BMJ Open* 7, no. 7 (2017).

Wibisono, C., Y. Probst, E. Neale, and L. Tapsell. "Changes in Diet Quality during a 12 Month Weight Loss Randomised Controlled Trial." *BMC Nutrition* 3, no. 38 (2017).

INDEX

Acknowledgments

I want to thank Destini Moody for her writing contributions and Alejandro Pinot for recipe development assistance.

About the Author

Manuel Villacorta, MS, RDN, is an internationally recognized, award-winning registered dietitian-nutritionist with over 18 years of experience. He is based in San Francisco and helps people worldwide virtually.

Manuel is one of the leading weight loss and nutrition experts in the United States and is the recipient of five Best Bay Area Nutritionist awards and the 2019 Influencer of the Year by the Produce for Better Health Foundation. He is also a spokesperson for numerous food commodities and an in-demand nutrition expert on local and national television and radio. He is a best-selling author, having published seven books.

Born and raised in Peru, he earned his bachelor's of science in nutrition and physiology metabolism from the University of California, Berkeley, and his master's of science in nutrition and food science from San Jose State University. He has been the recipient of numerous awards for his research and contributions to nutrition and dietetics.